An Inculturation Model
of the Catholic Marriage Ritual

An Inculturation Model of the Catholic Marriage Ritual

David William Antonio

A PUEBLO BOOK

The Liturgical Press   Collegeville Minnesota

A Pueblo Book published by The Liturgical Press

Design by Frank Kacmarcik, OBL.S.B. Cover illustration: detail, *The Wedding at Cana*, Esperanza Guevara, from *The Gospel in Art by the Peasants of Solentiname*, Orbis.

Library of Congress Cataloging-in-Publication Data

Antonio, David William, 1963–
  An inculturation model of the Catholic marriage ritual /
David William Antonio.
    p. cm.
  Includes bibliographical references and index.
  ISBN 0-8146-6186-6 (alk. paper)
    1. Marriage service—Philippines—Ilocos. 2. Catholic Church—
Philippines—Ilocos—Liturgy. 3. Ilokanos (Philippine people)—Marriage
customs and rites. I. Title.

BX2250 .A546 2002
264'.02085'095991—dc21   2002075278

Contents

Preface

It is my pleasure to present this work prepared by Fr. David William Antonio, priest of the Archdiocese of Nueva Segovia in the Ilocos region of the Northern Philippines.

Though prepared for a particular local church and its inhabitants, in its revised form the book should appeal to all who are interested in a fitting celebration of the Order of Marriage or in the task of liturgical inculturation. The first part of the book gives the reader a thorough presentation of the typical edition of the Order for the Celebration of Marriage as revised in 1991. The study allows us to see the theology of marriage included in this order, its principles of liturgical celebration, and its directives for the work of inculturation. This is of benefit for all interested in the celebration of marriage or indeed in a solidly based scriptural and liturgical catechesis of the sacrament and of family life.

With this sound investigation in hand, Father Antonio brings us on to consider the aims and method of liturgical inculturation. While he gives us an apt discussion of the Roman Instruction on Inculturation of 1994 and a summary of the work of his fellow countryman, Fr. Anscar Chupungco, o.s.b., he presents new and fresh insights through his study of the method of contextualization. This is of service not only to the order of marriage but to all work on bringing Christian liturgy into cultures and cultures into Christian liturgy.

The work on Ilocano customs and on the Ilocano ritual, as presented here, is greatly abbreviated. I could only do honor to the thorough, careful, and indeed fascinating contribution of the original dissertation. In this current shortened form, however, we have a good model, for we see the process at work and we are given universally applicable guidance on how to go about such a task. For a reader who is not of the local church of the Ilocos, one of the more interesting proposals is that of a continuous rite that brings a couple from engagement to marriage ceremony through different stages of catechesis and celebration. We are all aware of the advantages of such a continuous rite from the Order for the Initiation of Adults. We may also be aware of the difficulties encountered in preparing couples for marriage and of the need for some such order or rite. As a living example, Father Antonio's proposal will surely be of interest and benefit beyond the confines of its immediate public. That it attends so carefully to cultural realities is an added guide and challenge for any church. In North America, it may be of special help to minorities who are in quest of a liturgy that is respectful of their cultures and able to integrate their beliefs, customs, and "webs of significance."

David N. Power, O.M.I.
Professor Emeritus, The Catholic University of America

Acknowledgments

One of the deeper joys of writing and publishing this work is the opportunity it provides for remembering those who played important roles in its genesis, development, and completion.

A special word of thanks is due to Dr. David N. Power, O.M.I., a most esteemed mentor and friend, without whom this project would not have been completed. It was he who inspired and guided this work from "start to finish." I thank Dr. Michael Downey, who was instrumental in having the project brought to the consideration of The Liturgical Press. He and Dr. Richard Fragomeni, Dr. Kevin Irwin, and Dr. Margaret Mary Kelleher, O.S.U., gave me a lot of encouragement. Their insightful suggestions and constructive critique contributed greatly to the enrichment of the book.

Grateful acknowledgment goes to The Liturgical Press for the interest they have shown in publishing this work. I thank Mark Twomey, editorial director, Annette Kmitch, editor, and Colleen Stiller, production manager, for their exceptional patience and understanding.

The Most Rev. Orlando Quevedo, O.M.I., D.D., my former Ordinary who gave me the wonderful opportunity to do further studies, and the Most Rev. Edmundo M. Abaya, D.D., my present Ordinary, have always challenged me to offer my best to the Church. I shall forever be grateful to them and the Clergy of Nueva Segovia for their unflagging support and trust.

Over the years, the community at the Immaculate Conception School of Theology in Vigan City, particularly the members of the faculty, has been a constant source of inspiration and encouragement. Dr. Bernhard Raas, S.V.D., a former seminary professor, deserves special mention. It was he who first introduced me to and nurtured my interest in the study of liturgy.

I owe a special debt of gratitude to all my friends whose prayers and reassuring words have made priestly ministry, especially in the seminary context, less trying. They have done me more kindnesses than I can repay.

I cannot possibly end this list without mentioning my parents, brothers and sister, and their families. They may not share my theological and liturgical interests but their much-needed support in what I love doing has never been wanting. In their own simple and unobtrusive ways they have taught me what it means to be a culturally-rooted Christian. *Dios ti agngina!*

Introduction

This book is the reworking of a doctoral dissertation done at The Catholic University of America, Washington, D.C., under the direction of Fr. David Noel Power, O.M.I. Materials from the dissertation have now been revised with his help to make it suitable for a wider readership.

In 1991 the Roman Congregation for Divine Worship and the Discipline of Sacraments published a revision of the post–Vatican II Order for the Celebration of Marriage (hereafter ROCM). Though not yet published in English translation, it can make a significant contribution to the celebration and to the inculturation of marriage rites. In the dissertation, my purpose was to prepare the proposal of a marriage rite, in the native language of the people, that could be considered for use in the dioceses of the region of the Ilocos in the Northern Philippines. While the work did conclude with such a proposal, prepared in detail, the preparation meant a close study of the revised Roman Ritual and of the marriage customs and practices of the Ilocano people.

In the work here presented, the first two chapters are an essay in liturgical theology. They analyze and comment upon the rites and texts of the rite promulgated in 1991. The rite includes directives for the preparation of regional texts, adapted to the cultures of different peoples. Hence the third chapter discusses the principles and methods of liturgical inculturation and contextualization. The remaining part of the book treats, much more briefly than the original dissertation, the investigation into Ilocano customs and the composition of a liturgical ritual suited to the Ilocano people. In its shortened form, it is my hope that it will serve as a working model for peoples of other cultures who have to do similar liturgical preparation. This may be particularly true for churches, on whatever continent, whose membership includes peoples who knew an era of colonialism but never lost the riches of their own cultures in the fusion of cultures and beliefs that followed.

Chapter I

The 1991 Roman Order for the Celebration of Marriage

The purpose of this chapter is to present and analyze the Roman Order for the Celebration of Marriage (ROCM) in the typical edition of the 1991 order, so as to uncover its theological, pastoral, and liturgical orientations. This revision of the order already promulgated in 1969 needs to be seen in the context of the proposals approved by the Second Vatican Council and of the experience of marriage ceremonies that evolved between the two editions. A second chapter will be devoted to a study of its lectionary and prayer texts.

THE REVISION IN CONTEXT

A constitutive part of Vatican II's agenda of liturgical renewal was the reform of all sacramental rites, which includes the work of correcting, improving, revising, or updating, when necessary, the liturgical texts and rites of the sacraments. The Constitution on the Liturgy devoted two articles to the reform of the rites of marriage (articles 77, 78).

The first paragraph of article 77 mandated the revision and enrichment of the rite of celebrating marriage in the Roman Ritual, "in such a way that it will express more clearly the grace of the sacrament, and emphasize the duties of wife and husband."[1] In the judgment of the Council Fathers, the Roman Rite promulgated by Pope Paul V in 1614 and still in use before the council did not adequately express the grace of the sacrament and the obligation of the spouses in spite of the modifications introduced by Popes Benedict XIV (1752), Pius IX (1872), Leo

---

[1] See *Decrees of the Ecumenical Councils,* vol. II, ed. and trans. Norman P. Tanner (Washington, D.C.: Sheed & Ward, and Georgetown University Press, 1990) 834.

XIII (1884), Pius XI (1925), and Pius XII (1952).[2] It was considered too juridical in orientation since it viewed marriage primarily as a contract. The celebration proposed by the Roman Ritual was too short, too dry, and too sober to have an impact or leave a lasting impression, so that many of the bishops during the discussions prior to the council lamented its brevity as well as its symbolic and ritual poverty.[3]

It had not been the intention of the Council of Trent to suppress all local customs, and the Roman Rite of 1614 was only intended as a model for local rituals. Thus the second paragraph of article 77 of the Constitution quotes directly from the Council of Trent, which called for the retention and preservation of "other praiseworthy customs and ceremonies used in other regions."[4] In the long run, however, the Roman Rite of 1614 supplanted the local rituals in many regions, and local customs turned into appendices to the Roman Ritual. Despite this process of "romanization," local rituals survived in Spain,[5] France, Milan, and Germany.[6] In other cases, the Roman ritual was adapted to include elements from medieval rites.

The third paragraph in article 77 of the Constitution granted each conference of bishops the faculty to "draw up its own rite suited to its people and region, in accordance with the provisions of article 63." This paragraph manifests great flexibility and openness. It does not merely allow the insertion or integration of good, laudable, and honorable indigenous marriage ceremonies into particular rituals, nor does it simply permit the adaptation of the *editio typica* to local marriage customs and traditions. More significantly, it endows bishops, even of nonmissionary

[2] See Cyrille Vogel, *Medieval Liturgy: An Introduction to the Sources,* trans. and rev. William Storey and Niels Rasmussen (Washington, D.C.: Pastoral Press, 1986) 264–5, 271.

[3] Anscar Chupungco, *Liturgies of the Future: The Process and Methods of Inculturation* (New York: Paulist Press, 1989) 118. Ricardo Serrano, in his study "Towards a Cultural Adaptation of the Rite of Marriage" (S.L.D. dissertation, Pontifical Institute of Liturgy, 1987), presents an interesting list of the conciliar Fathers who deplored the poverty and juridicism of the Roman Ritual and strongly lobbied for its revision. See especially pp. 6–9.

[4] See Concilium Tridentinum, Sessio XXIV, Decretum *De Reformatione,* cap. 1, in Tanner, *Decrees,* vol. II, 756. This principle is echoed in Paul V's *Rituale Romanum,* tit. VII, cap. 2, n. 6.

[5] See Dionisio Borobio, *Inculturación del matrimonio* (Madrid: San Pablo, 1993) 67–73.

[6] See Kenneth Stevenson, *Nuptial Blessing* (New York: Oxford University Press, 1983) 172–7.

regions, with the faculty to create new marriage rites proper to their own regions. The only requirement, reduced to the bare minimum, is the juridical requisite for validity; namely, that the priest assisting at the marriage asks for and obtains the consent of the contracting parties.

Complementing the preceding article, article 78 specifies the operational principles for the revision of the typical edition of the marriage rite. First, it demands that normally the sacrament is to be celebrated within Mass. This is meant to underscore the close relationship between the two sacraments. Second, it asks that the nuptial blessing, which may be said in the vernacular, be revised so as to constitute a blessing for the couple and not only for the bride, as had been the tradition of the Roman liturgy hitherto. The revised blessing should remind both spouses of their equal obligation of mutual fidelity. The nuptial blessing was originally a prayer for the bride alone. Third, if the sacrament is celebrated outside the Mass, a Liturgy of the Word is to precede it and the nuptial blessing should always be given. This is counter to the practice which allowed for the blessing only within a Mass, as well as the prohibition to give the blessing to widows who remarry.

On March 19, 1969, the Sacred Congregation of Rites officially promulgated the typical edition of the revised marriage rites which would serve as foundation for the texts and rites of local rituals. It is a ritual that is said to embody the enriched conciliar theology of marriage as well as the liturgical reforms it envisioned. The introduction (nos. 1–18) provides the rite's theological, liturgical, and pastoral orientations. This situates the celebration within a renewed theology of the sacrament of marriage that is more christological and ecclesial, as well as sensitive to contemporary pastoral and anthropological issues.

The rite of marriage within Mass in the 1969 typical edition has the following structure. It begins with an introductory rite, preferably at the church door, where the priest receives and welcomes the couple, their relatives, and friends. He may lead them in procession to their designated places. The Liturgy of the Word follows the opening prayer. After the homily, the liturgy of the sacrament or marriage rite proper is celebrated, in which the minister questions the couple about their freedom, intention to remain faithful, and the acceptance of their responsibility for children from the marriage. With hands joined, the couple express their mutual consent and the minister receives it. The blessing and giving of rings follow. The Liturgy of the Eucharist follows with the possibility of having the bride and groom present the eucharistic gifts. Immediately after the Lord's Prayer and before the kiss of peace, the nuptial blessing is given to the couple, replacing the embolism *Libera nos.* Communion is given to the bride and groom in both species. To conclude the rite a solemn blessing is pronounced over them after the post-communion prayer.[7]

What is very significant in this ritual is the restoration of the infrangible link between the Word of God and the sacrament. The introduction of a Liturgy of the Word which, as in other sacramental celebrations, precedes the sacrament itself, even when it is not celebrated within the Mass, is praiseworthy.[8] This ritual makes provision for three readings and demands that a homily be given, preferably by the presider.[9]

In sharp contrast to its immediate predecessor, this typical edition (1969) is characterized by a richer theological content, a nobler liturgical shape, and a very liberal or flexible attitude toward liturgical adaptation. Old and new elements have been put together in the creation of a ritual that attempts to satisfy the demands of liturgical reform and contemporary needs. Some of these old elements, such as those which belong to the old rite of marriage (interrogation and the giving of consent, reception of consent by the priest, blessing and handing over of wedding rings, nuptial and closing blessings) have been reworked and retouched to correspond with the shifts in theological and liturgical understanding of the sacrament. New texts and formulas have been composed and added to further enrich the ritual.

Enriched by biblical rather than juridical concepts, a paradigm shift is evident in the ritual. From an understanding of marriage viewed as contract *(contractus)* the text moves to a view of the union as covenant *(foedus).*[10] While there is still talk of procreation and education of children as a goal in marriage, other aspects, such as companionship, the human and Christian relation of the couple, or their mutual gift of self, are also given attention. Less emphasis is given to the role of the priest and greater accent is put on the primary role of the bride and groom as the true ministers of the sacrament.[11]

[7] This was in the 1969 order, nos. 19–38.

[8] Adrien Nocent, "Le rituel du mariage depuis Vatican II," *La celebrazione cristiana del matrimonio: Simboli e testi,* ed. G. Farnedi (Rome: Pontificio Ateneo S. Anselmo, 1986) 130.

[9] The term "presider" refers to the one who leads the liturgical celebration; namely, a priest or deacon or a duly designated layperson.

[10] See, for example, nos. 2, 6, and 33 of the 1969 order.

[11] Note, for example, the change in the formula of receiving the consent: The 1614 Ritual has the priest say, *Ego conjungo vos . . .* while making a gesture of

In spite of the positive developments exhibited by the 1969 ritual, it was not seen as a perfect text. Some theologians and liturgists pointed out a number of its deficiencies or limitations.[12] It has no true epiclesis or invocation of the Spirit, either by gesture or by word, that would express the relationship between marriage and the Holy Spirit, who makes the union and fidelity to the bond possible. Along with this, the ecclesial dimension of the marriage celebration is underdeveloped. The liturgical assembly is not granted enough opportunities to exercise its common priesthood through a more active participation in the rites. Authors also lament that in spite of the revisions and reworking of texts and formulas, they still lack a true biblical orientation that captures in simple form the mystery of marriage and its theological sense in relation to the union of Christ and the Church. Moreover, the ritual does not seem to have sufficiently taken into account the contemporary cultural anthropology of marriage. Sensitive issues and values like fidelity, equality, respect for each other's rights, collaboration in all of the tasks within the family, and participation in the life of the larger society were not seriously addressed. Given these deficiencies, there are those who think that the 1969 ritual did not successfully distance itself from a juridical mentality.[13] It was also asked whether the changing social conditions of married life in this century needed to be taken more fully into account.

THE 1991 REVISED ORDER

Exactly twenty-one years after promulgation of the 1969 marriage ordo (March 19, 1991), the Congregation for Divine Worship and the Discipline of the Sacraments by the decree "Ritus celebrandi Matrimonium," promulgated and published a second edition of the Order of Celebrating Marriage for the Roman Rite.

---

blessing, which seems to suggest the central role of the priest. The 1969 ordo, however, does not tell the priest to make any gesture of blessing at this point but only to say the formula, no. 25 of the ritual.

[12] See, for instance, Borobio, *Inculturación del matrimonio*, 132–5; C. Carideo, "Teología della celebrazione liturgica del matrimonio cristiano," *La celebrazione del matrimonio cristiano* (Bologna: Edizioni Dehoniane, 1977) 163–202; Adrien Nocent, "Le rituel du mariage depuis Vatican II," *La celebrazione cristiana del matrimonio,* ed. G. Farnedi (Rome: Pontificio Ateneo S. Anselmo, 1986) 129–44; Kenneth Stevenson, *To Join Together: The Rite of Marriage* (New York: Pueblo Publishing Co., 1987) 136–61.

[13] See the comments of Nocent, "Le rituel du mariage," 133–4.

This second typical edition is not an entirely new liturgical book. Nor is it a mere reprint of the first edition. Rather, it is a typical edition which is an enrichment, an updating of its predecessor, introducing some significant changes as well as affirming the themes which have been proposed previously. It has also tried to remedy some of the deficiencies or lacunae found in the previous rite. In the realization of this ordo, much had been learned from the experience of other countries and their rituals. Likewise, new insights of the post-conciliar reflection on marriage and family life, such as those found in Pope John Paul II's apostolic exhortation on the family, *Familiaris Consortio* (1980),[14] and in the 1983 Code of Canon Law,[15] have greatly influenced it. The table below shows, in outline form, the points of convergence between the two editions as well as some of the new elements that have been introduced in the revised ritual.

As the table below shows, quantitatively and qualitatively, the new edition has been expanded with the introduction of new elements. ROCM has 286 articles compared to OCM's 127. The second typical edition has added a new chapter (Chapter III, on the Celebration of Marriage Before a Lay Minister), and three appendices (Sample General Intercessions, Order for the Blessing of an Engaged Couple, Order for the Blessing of a Married Couple within Mass on the An-

1969 Order	1991 Order
General Introduction (*praenotanda*): 1–18	General Introduction: 1–44
Chapter I Rite of Marriage within Mass: 19–38	Chapter I Rite of Marriage within Mass: 45–78
Chapter II Rite of Marriage Outside Mass: 39–54	Chapter II Rite of Marriage Outside Mass: 79–117
Chapter III Marriage Between a Catholic and an Unbaptized Person: 55–66	Chapter III Celebration of Marriage Before a Lay Minister: 118–51

[14] *AAS* 74 (1982) 143–65.

[15] Texts and translation in *Code of Canon Law,* Latin-English Edition (Washington, D.C.: Canon Law Society of America, 1983). Hereafter this will be quoted as CIC.

1969 Order	1991 Order
Chapter IV Optional Texts in the Marriage Rite and in the Wedding Mass: 67–127	Chapter IV Marriage Between a Catholic and a Catechumen or Non-Christian: 152–78
	Chapter V Various Texts for Marriage Rite and Nuptial Mass: 179–250
	Appendices: I. Sample General Intercessions: 251–2 II. Order for the Blessing of an Engaged Couple: 253–71 III. Order for the Blessing of a Married Couple within Mass on the Anniversary of Marriage: 272–86

niversary of Marriage).[16] These additions reveal the intention and goal of the revised edition to respond more faithfully to contemporary pastoral realities. New texts have been added to the options already provided in the older edition. Choices are now given for the welcome address or initial exhortation (nos. 52–3). There is a new alternative formula for the reception of consent (nos. 64). An acclamation after the exchange of consent has been provided (nos. 65, 99, 133, 164). The possibility of singing a hymn after the exchange of rings is now offered (nos. 68, 102, 136, 168). A preeminent modification is the inclusion of a more pronounced pneumatology in the introduction to the rite (no. 9) and in the nuptial blessing where the invocation for the grace of the Holy Spirit is inserted (nos. 74, 140, 172, 242, 244). The formulas for the nuptial blessing have also been reworked so as to include both spouses. Where it is customary, the signing of the marriage register may take place during the ceremony, but this is not to be done at the altar (nos. 78, 117, 151, 178). Some helpful rubrics have been added to facilitate the celebration (nos. 53, 72). Of special interest is the provision of a service for betrothal, whose use can put preparation for marriage in a liturgical setting.

---

[16] A more detailed study of these new additions will be made later in the chapter.

THE GENERAL INTRODUCTION

In every typical edition of the rites of the liturgy the General Introduction offers a great help in understanding the meaning of the sacrament celebrated. Not only does it aid pastors or pastoral agents and the faithful in making careful preparations for the celebration, but it also presents the theological aspects highlighted by the rite itself. In other words, it presents the general theological, liturgical, and pastoral orientations of the rite concerned. That is to say, it gives the points of departure for theological reflection and liturgical-pastoral praxis.[17] Our interest is in what the introduction says about the theology of marriage, the offices and ministries involved, the shape of liturgies which are suggested, and the ritual adaptations envisioned.

THE THEOLOGY OF MARRIAGE

The introduction to the 1969 Order for the Celebration of Marriage had already included mention of the covenant quality of marriage, putting an accent on the bond of fidelity and on marriage as a moment in salvation history. These features of the theology of marriage are considerably expanded in the 1991 revision of this ritual. Compared to the ordo of 1969 the second typical edition presents a richer exposition of the Church's teachings on marriage.

Marriage and Creation

The introduction develops an insight which is not well-elaborated in the 1969 ritual, that is, marriage finds its foundation in creation. It asserts that the marriage union derives its power and strength from the ordering of creation (no. 1). Marriage is a reality in the life of humanity even before the coming of Christ. Yet it was God, not human beings, who established this "intimate communion of life and love" (no. 4) between a man and a woman. God has meant them to live in a life-long bond with each other (no. 1). God has also willed that this union be possessed of special blessings and purposes (no. 4). For this reason matrimony is a way of cooperating in the love and work of God, the Creator. This theological concept has very important implications. It is a break with theology's earlier insistence on the tainting of marriage with sin. Embracing the notion that marriage is intrinsically good, insofar as it was God who willed it, should be the *coup de grace* to the idea that marriage is, in our present state, a remedy for concupiscence.

---

[17] José Rodriguez, "Nueva Edición del Ritual del Matrimonio," *Phase* 187 (1992) 14.

Marriage as a Partnership of Life between Husband and Wife

This is one of the aspects given stress in the new edition. Marriage is a partnership of life between a man and a woman, a result of the choice made by both. This implies a mutual acceptance in all openness and liberty. The irrevocable consent they give to each other in the establishment of the conjugal covenant is a truly free human act (nos. 1 and 2). This natural or anthropological union between husband and wife, for the purpose of companionship and the begetting and education of children, is in harmony with the will of the Creator-God. What is emphasized is the partners' mutual consent and relationship.

Marriage: Raised by Christ to the Dignity of a Sacrament

This is given greater emphasis here in this revised version of the order. Christ the Lord "restored marriage to its primordial form and holiness" and "raised it to the dignity of a sacrament, modeled on his own nuptial bond with the Church" (no. 5). His presence at the wedding in Cana (John 2:1-11) is understood as a confirmation of the goodness of marriage and the proclamation that from thereon marriage is an efficacious sign of Christ's presence. The changing of water into wine became a sign of the new covenant. As God once entered into a covenant of love and fidelity with the people of Israel, so Christ the bridegroom has brought the Church as his bride into a new and everlasting covenant, through his paschal mystery (no. 6).[18] This covenant between Christ and the Church is signified and realized in the sacrament of matrimony (no. 8). This is the fundamental christological dimension of Christian marriage.

Marriage and the Church

The ecclesial aspect of the sacrament is another theme given more space in the revised edition. By reason of baptism, the sacrament of faith, a man and a woman are once and for all brought into the covenant between Christ and the Church, so that their marital communion is assumed into Christ's own love and enriched by the power of his sacrifice. As a sacrament of initiation, baptism radically inserts us into the mystery of the covenantal relationship between Christ and the Church. In marriage the couple acts out of the covenantal relationship already established in baptism. This is the so-called baptismal foundation of marriage. The reason why marriage is a sacrament is that it is the act of

---

[18] See also *Gaudium et Spes* 48.

two persons who through baptism have already entered a paschal and covenantal relationship with Christ (nos. 7–8). The universal call to holiness (LG 5) is given concrete expression in marriage. It finds its foundation in the salvific initiative and action of God in Christ,[19] which is first expressed in baptism but now taken up in marriage.

The Holy Spirit in Marriage[20]

As mentioned earlier, one of the most notable features of the new ordo is the inclusion of a pneumatology. There is now a recognition of the principal role of the Holy Spirit in the making of a marriage as well as in its success. Article 9 of the introduction calls upon Christian spouses to follow the example of Christ "who loved the Church and gave himself for his bride" (Eph 5:25). It also reminds them of the other demands of Christian married life: "to strive to nurture and foster their marriage in an equal dignity, with mutual self-giving and undivided love that flow from the divine font of charity." It makes clear, however, that the realization of these demands is the work of the Holy Spirit, mediated by the grace of the sacrament, rather than the result of human effort alone. It is the Holy Spirit who keeps their love and unity in Christ. It is the same Spirit who makes it possible that the total love of Christ for the Church is made manifest or even approximated in the real life of married Christians, that is, in unwavering mutual fidelity, in good times and in bad, shunning all adultery and divorce.

Marriage as a Participation in God's Work and a Call to Witness to His Love

Quoting *Gaudium et Spes* 50, number 10 of the General Introduction makes reference to procreation and education of children as one of the purposes of marriage and conjugal love. "Without detraction from the other ends of marriage . . . married Christians should be steadfast and ready to cooperate with the love of the Creator and Savior, who through them will constantly enrich and enlarge his own family" (no. 10). This office of procreation, rooted in conjugal love and communion in life, is a participation in God's creative work. The fulfillment of this office as well as the holy manner of the couple's lives serve to glorify God.

[19] Rodriguez, "Nueva Edición," 17.

[20] For a more thorough discussion on the pneumatological aspect of the sacrament of Marriage see A. M. Triacca, "Spiritus Sancti virtutis infusio," *Notitiae* 288 (1991) 365–90.

God who called the couple to marriage continues to call them throughout marriage "to make progress in it . . . to celebrate effectively with faith in God's word the mystery of Christ and the Church, to live rightly, and to bear witness in the eyes of all" (no. 11).

OFFICES AND MINISTRIES

Compared with its predecessor, the new typical edition is more comprehensive in scope and more specific in identifying offices and ministries involved in the preparation and celebration of marriage. In fact, it dedicates sixteen articles to this subject.

The Couples and Their Families

Echoing *Familiaris Consortio* 66, ROCM 12 states that although on the grounds of pastoral and liturgical care the preparation and celebration of marriage concerns the bishop, the parish priest (pastor) and his assistants, and, at least to some degree, the entire ecclesial community, it concerns above all the future spouses themselves and their families.[21] Giving the couples the primary responsibility is an important theological and pastoral point. It corresponds well with the doctrine that they themselves are the ministers of the sacrament. It also implies that they themselves have grown in faith within their families and are thus ready for marriage. Working closely with their pastors and other ministers, engaged couples are to observe all the requirements for validly and lawfully contracting marriage. They are to undergo catechesis on the elements of Christian teaching, particularly on marriage and the family, on the sacrament itself and its rites, prayers, and readings (no. 17). Together with their pastors, they help determine the shape of the liturgical celebration by choosing the readings, the form of expressing their mutual consent, the texts for the blessing of rings, for the nuptial blessing, for the intentions of the general intercessions, and the songs (no. 29). As far as possible, they are to make sure that they complete their Christian initiation before they receive the sacrament of marriage (no. 18).[22] It is recommended that the couple receive the sacrament of reconciliation to prepare themselves spiritually for the celebration of their marriage within the Eucharist.

[21] While article 12 does not specify how the family may be involved in the preparations, it makes reference to *Familias Consortio* 23, which maintains that the family should be involved in the remote, proximate, and immediate preparations for marriage.

[22] This simply repeats the norm prescribed in CIC, can. 1065, paragraphs 1 and 2.

The Bishop

The bishop, as the pastor of the local church, is to regulate the celebration and pastoral care of the sacrament, and to offer Christians the help by which the marriage state is safeguarded, taking into account any norms or pastoral guidelines issued by the conference of bishops regarding preparation of couples or pastoral care of marriage (no. 13). He sees to it that "apart from the liturgical laws providing honors to civil authorities, there is to be no preferential treatment of any private persons or classes of persons" (no. 31).[23] In places where there is a lack of priests or deacons, it is also the bishop who, "after a prior favorable decision of the conference of bishops and with the permission of the Apostolic See, delegates laypersons to assist at marriages" (no. 25).[24]

The Pastor

A very important office and ministry is that of the pastor (with the help of his assistants), who has to ensure that the assistance needed by the community in regard to marriage is provided. Paragraph 14 enumerates four ways in which this assistance is to be given. First of all, through preaching and catechesis the faithful are instructed on the meaning of Christian marriage and on the duty of Christian spouses and parents. Second, through personal preparation for those entering marriage, they are prepared for the holiness and duties of their new state. The pastor is to welcome engaged couples, and since the sacrament of marriage presupposes and demands faith, he is to cultivate and foster their faith (no. 16). Third, through an effective liturgical celebration, the meaning of the sacramental liturgy may clearly stand out. Fourth, through the assistance provided for those already married, they may succeed in living within the family a life that is more holy and full, as they faithfully preserve and safeguard the marriage bond.

In relation to the abovementioned, the pastor, "taking into account the attitudes of the people toward marriage and the family, must endeavor to evangelize in the light of faith a mutual and genuine love between the couple" (no. 20). He is to make sure that the requirements of law for validly and lawfully contracting marriage are observed (nos. 20 and 22). On certain occasions, he must make judgments on the admission or nonadmission of couples to the cele-

[23] See *Sacrosanctum Concilium* 34.
[24] See CIC, can. 1112, §§ 1–2.

bration of the sacrament (no. 21). The pastor or the priest who prepares the couple is the one preferred to give the homily during the celebration, receive the consent of the spouses, and celebrate the Mass (no. 23). Finally, the pastor may also give to a deacon the faculty to preside at the celebration of marriage (no. 24).

The Deacon

The deacon may also preside at the celebration of the sacrament, including bestowing the nuptial blessing, after he has received a faculty from the pastor or the local Ordinary (no. 24).[25]

Lay Minister

A significant change introduced by the new ordo is the possibility for a layperson to assist at marriages, that is, to ask and receive the consent of the spouses in the name of the Church and to lead the liturgical service. As we have seen above, number 25 speaks of the faculty given to diocesan bishops to empower suitable laypersons who will assist in marriages, where there is a lack of priests or deacons. Their suitability has to be based on their capability to instruct engaged couples and to carry out the marriage liturgy rightly. Other laypersons can also have a part in the preparation of couples.

The Community

ROCM mentions the important role of the community in helping to spiritually prepare the couples and to actively participate in the ritual celebration. Laypersons, aside from those delegated to assist at marriages, can have a part in both the spiritual preparation of the couples and in the celebration of the rite (no. 26). Marriage has a communal character and calls for the participation of the parish community, at least in the person of some of its members (no. 28). Likewise, the entire Christian community is to cooperate in bearing witness to the faith, showing before the world the love of Christ (no. 26).

Indeed, we can appreciate here the way the new ordo has retrieved the communal dimension of the marriage celebration. With the greatest possible participation of the Christian community from the preparation up to the actual celebration, this new ritual has really come a long way from the sober, short, and juridical Roman Ritual of 1614.

[25] The text refers to CIC, can. 1111.

PREPARATION AND CELEBRATION OF THE LITURGY

The revised rite discusses the preparations needed for the liturgy of marriage in five articles (nos. 28–32). The first thing that captures our attention is its accent on the communitarian orientation of this task. Unlike the 1969 ordo which seems to leave all the work to the pastor, the text of 1991 declares that since marriage is meant to increase and sanctify the people of God, "its celebration has a communal character that calls for the participation even of the parish community, at least in the person of some of its members." It is due to this communal dimension that celebrating marriages during the Sunday assembly or having several marriages at the same time may be considered, if the occasion suggests it or it is not against local customs (no. 28b).

It is urged that pastors prepare the celebration, as far as possible, with the prospective spouses. Together they are to choose, from among the various options provided, "the readings that will be explained in the homily; the form for expressing mutual consent; the texts for the blessing of rings, for the nuptial blessing, for the intentions of the general intercessions, and for singing." Moreover, upon the recommendation of the pastor and with his guidance, the couples help determine the form of celebration, whether it be the one for use within Mass or another. The instructions for celebration are mindful of the impact of music and liturgical space. Appropriate songs are to be chosen, with special attention to the responsorial psalm (no. 30). Suitable decoration of the church should be considered, avoiding, however, any form of social discrimination among couples (no. 31). With regard to the choice of marriage date, the new ordo makes clear that any day except Good Friday and Holy Saturday is possible. The only request is that spouses respect the nature of days with penitential character (such as during Lent)[26] when marriage is celebrated at such times.

THE CHOICE OF RITE TO BE USED

The revised ordo dedicates six paragraphs (nos. 33–38) to the choice of rite to be used in various circumstances, elaborating further on issues already taken up in 1969. As in the 1969 edition, the distinction is made between a marriage within Mass and outside Mass, with their corresponding rites. These are given in Chapter I (within Mass) when both parties are baptized Catholics, and Chapter II (outside Mass)

---

[26] This repeats the 1969 text, no. 11b.

when a Catholic and a baptized non-Catholic are involved. Number 35 repeats earlier provisions concerning the possibility of celebrating the rite within Mass in the case of a mixed marriage (Catholic and baptized non-Catholic). It also offers guidelines with regard to a marriage between a Catholic and a catechumen or a non-Christian (Chapter IV).

The 1991 text parallels number 6 of 1969, which deals with the main elements of the marriage celebration that are to be given prominence (i.e., Liturgy of the Word, consent of the parties, the nuptial blessing, and eucharistic Communion). A few modifications on the paragraph can, however, be noted. For example, there is now a reference to the nuptial blessing as "an ancient prayer by which the blessing of God is invoked upon the bride and groom." The new rite reminds pastors that special attention needs to be given to those, whether Catholics or non-Catholics, who never or hardly ever take part in a celebration of marriage or Eucharist. This applies above all to the spouses themselves (no. 37). Finally, an instruction is given in number 38 that, in addition to the requisites for the celebration of the Mass, the ritual book and the rings for the spouses should be prepared ahead of the celebration in the sanctuary, and when necessary a vessel of holy water with sprinkler and a communion cup should be available.

ON ADAPTATION OF THE RITE

Here it is appropriate to recall the provisions already made in the 1969 order for the celebration of marriage, which was supposed to apply the conciliar reform and offer guidelines for the adaptation of the marriage rite to both the pastoral and cultural needs of the people.[27] This expectation was met with a certain degree of satisfaction. The order offered a wide range of options and possibilities that include structure as well as content. Numbers 12 to 16 of the introduction to the rite correspond to articles 63b and 77 of the Constitution on the Liturgy and deal with the preparation of particular rituals, while numbers 17 and 18 speak of the faculty granted to the conferences of bishops to compose a completely new rite of marriage, according to the third principle of article 77.[28]

---

[27] Anscar Chupungco, "The Cultural Adaptation of the Rite of Marriage," *La celebrazione cristiana del matrimonio,* Analecta Liturgica 11 (Rome: Pontificio Ateneo S. Anselmo, 1986) 154.

[28] Ibid.

Preparation of Particular Rituals

The 1969 ordo essentially harks back to the principles enunciated in the Council of Trent[29] and Vatican II and calls for the preparation of particular rituals "suitable for the customs and needs of individual areas" (no. 12), on the basis of the Roman typical edition. Local churches, however, also have the freedom to compose a completely new rite. The ordo mentions some options and possibilities. Number 13 gives the option to adapt or supplement formularies of the Roman ritual, "including the questions before the consent and the actual words of consent." When the Roman ritual has a number of optional formulas, local rituals may add other formulas of the same type. This means that local churches may creatively compose new texts that satisfy the requirements of both liturgy and culture.

Numbers 14 and 15 allow flexibility and variation in the arrangement of the parts of the celebration and in the use of what we call "explanatory rites." Elements like the exhortation, the exchange of consent, the blessing and exchange of rings, and the nuptial blessing can be rearranged to suit the local needs.[30] The only requirement that has to be observed is for the priest to ask and receive the consent of the contracting parties. In accord with local customs, the explanatory rite of crowning or veiling the bride after the exchange of rings may take place. But "in any region where the joining of the hands or the blessing and exchange of rings does not fit in with the practice of the people, they may be omitted or substituted with other rites." It is clear then that the ordo manifests cultural sensitivity and therefore encourages the use of explanatory rites rooted in the culture of the people or, at least, in harmony with it.

Besides the aforementioned, number 16 of the General Introduction shows a liberal attitude toward the incorporation of native customs in the missions. Citing the provisions of *Sacrosanctum Concilium* 37, it sees the possibility of taking over these marriage customs into the Christian celebration of marriage, provided these customs and traditions are "not indissolubly bound up with superstition and error," and as long as they can be made to "harmonize with the true and authentic spirit of the liturgy." Anscar Chupungco makes the comment that number 16 deals with the preparation of particular rituals on the basis of the *editio typica*. The method of adaptation envisaged here is

[29] See Tanner, *Decrees,* vol. II, 756.
[30] Chupungco, "Cultural Adaptation of Marriage," 157.

that of acculturation, which means that suitable elements borrowed from indigenous marriage rites are given a Christian meaning and inserted in the particular ritual.[31]

Preparation of a Completely New Rite

Applying the third principle of article 77 of the Constitution on the Liturgy, which allows the creation of new marriage rites independent of the *editio typica*, numbers 17 and 18 of the General Introduction see the possibility of preparing a completely new rite. Despite the kind of liberal attitude displayed by the *editio typica* toward the preparation of particular rituals, the results may not be enough to truly respond to the needs of the local churches. There is a recognition that some communities, especially in the missions, possess rich marriage rites which, when adapted and given Christian meaning, can even surpass the Roman Rite itself. Three conditions are given for the preparation of a new rite. The first requires that in the rite the priest (or the suitable witness) assisting at such a marriage asks for and receives the consent of the contracting parties. The second demands that the nuptial blessing be given at all times. The third dictates the submission of the rite to the Apostolic See for review and approval. What we have here is a possibility of inculturation or radical adaptation whereby indigenous marriage rites are creatively adopted resulting in a completely new rite.

Number 18 concerns situations such as in missionary areas, "where marriage ceremonies customarily take place in the home, sometimes over a period of several days." It makes the suggestion that these customs be adapted to the Christian spirit and to the liturgy. In these cases, "conferences of bishops, according to the pastoral needs of the people, may allow the sacramental rite to be celebrated in the home." This provision is clearly a response to the need of bringing the sacrament closer to native customs so that the sacramental rite can begin "to incarnate itself in the socio-cultural and religious traditions of the people."[32]

The 1991 Text

In speaking of adaptations, the revised text practically repeats what has been said in the first edition, although some reorganization has

[31] Ibid., 158.
[32] Ibid., 160.

been made as well as an attempt to concretize the provisions, specifying how they may be applied.

Invoking the provisions of the Constitution on the Liturgy (nos. 37–40 and 63b), number 39 of the introduction repeats number 12 of the earlier ritual, indicating the competence of the conferences of bishops in making adaptations of the new ritual for use in their own regions. In number 40 the new edition further identifies the responsibilities of the episcopal conferences in this regard. First, they are to determine, from the ones indicated in the *prænotanda*, the adaptations to be made. Second, in order to achieve the conscious and active participation of all, they may adapt and supplement the General Introduction (from no. 36 on). Third, they are to prepare translations of the texts, so that they are truly adapted to the genius of the different languages and cultures, and to add, whenever appropriate, suitable melodies for singing. Fourth, in preparing editions, they are to arrange the material in a form suitable for pastoral use.

Number 41 develops numbers 12–15 of the first typical edition. It gives certain guidelines for the drawing up of adaptations. The first and second guidelines refer to the possibility of adapting, supplementing, or even adding alternative texts to the Roman ritual, when circumstances suggest it. The third guideline speaks of the permissibility of reordering the parts of the rite, on the condition that the structure of the rite is maintained. Even the questions before the consent, if deemed suitable, may be omitted, provided the priest or whoever is officially assisting in the marriage asks for and receives the consent of the spouses. The fourth guideline speaks of the competence of the episcopal conference to rule, if demanded by pastoral need, that the consent of the contracting parties is always asked for by questioning. Guidelines five and six deal with the possibility of adding local customs such as the crowning of the bride or the veiling of bride and groom after the exchange of consent. Wherever the suggested rites in the Roman ritual are incongruous and not in harmony with the culture, such as joining of hands or the blessing and exchange of rings, they can be omitted or supplanted by other rites. The seventh guideline emphasizes the possibility of using elements in the tradition and culture of people in preparing new rites. It adds, however, that prudence is to be exercised in going about this work of adaptation.

Number 42 repeats number 17 of 1969 on the possibility for the episcopal conference to prepare and use, with the approval of the

Apostolic See, a completely new rite suited to their people and their culture, with the necessary conditions being observed. An added requirement, however, is that the General Introduction to the typical edition of the Roman Ritual be prefixed in this proper ritual (no. 43). Finally, number 44 sees the possibility, particularly in mission areas, of celebrating marriage in the home and over a period of several days.

By way of summary therefore, we can speak of at least four different methods or ways in which the Roman Rite of marriage may be adapted, as suggested by the General Introduction. The first is the translation of the rites and the formularies of the typical edition into the different languages of the local churches. A second method is adding or supplementing the Roman ritual with suitable texts and rites from the culture and traditions of people. A third possible means is the substitution of rituals and formularies which are reflective of the people's culture and language. A fourth method, one which radically departs from all of those mentioned, is the possibility of creating a completely new rite.

There are, however, important principles that have to be observed in undertaking these tasks. One is the exercise of prudence so that only suitable or worthy cultural elements may be incorporated in the rite. A second has to do with the hierarchical nature of the Church. This means that since the work of adaptation properly belongs to episcopal conferences, formal attempts at adapting the rite should be done in coordination with them. Moreover, the General Introduction also insists on the need for the approval of the Apostolic See before any official rite could be used. A third concerns what is considered to be a central element of the sacrament of marriage. It is the demand that, however the rite is ordered or the texts formulated, the priest or whoever is officially and validly assisting in the rite asks for and receives the consent of the parties.

Indeed, the introduction to the order provides enough room for adaptation—a clear indication that in this new typical edition, even more so than in the first edition, concrete steps have been taken toward the realization of Vatican II's agenda of liturgical reform and renewal.

CONCLUSION

In this chapter we have noted the principles of revision, the principal structural changes in the order of 1991, the theology of marriage expressed in the introduction to the order, and the norms given for the order's adaptation to different cultures. In the next chapter we can begin to look at the rite itself.

Chapter II

The Rite for the Sacrament of Marriage

In this chapter, we examine what pertains to the ritual for sacrament of marriage itself, looked at within the fuller liturgical setting, to note the modifications and innovations introduced by the revisions of 1969 and 1991, as well as to discern some of their implications. We will also look at some additions that affect the celebration of this rite, especially the rite for a celebration in which a layperson is official witness and presider, and the rite for the engagement of a couple. A further chapter will be devoted to the scriptural and euchological texts of the complete liturgy.

We shall focus on the Order of Celebrating Marriage within the Mass (Chapter I) inasmuch as it has been designated as the normal way of celebrating marriages in the Latin Church (no. 29). Moreover, except for some characteristic components, most of the elements making up the other rites[1] are already contained in the rite within the Mass.

STRUCTURE OF THE RITE

We start with a brief overview of the ceremony. The Celebration of Marriage within Mass in the second typical edition begins with an Introductory Rite whereby the couple is welcomed by the priest either at the door of the church (nos. 45–46) or at their designated place within the church. After the greeting the priest makes an introduction using either of the two formulas provided in the rite or similar words.[2] Omitting the

---

[1] These are: Rite of Marriage Outside the Mass (Chapter II), Celebration of Marriage in the Presence of a Lay Assistant (Chapter III), and the Rite of Marriage Between a Catholic and a Catechumen or Non-Christian (Chapter IV).

[2] This is new to the 1991 order of celebration.

penitential rite, the opening prayer from the Sacramentary (Ritual Mass: Wedding), or from the texts provided in Chapter V, is then said.

For the Liturgy of the Word, number 55 says that three readings may be proclaimed, the first of which must be taken from the Old Testament, except during the Easter season when it is taken from the book of Revelation. The directive adds that at least one reading should be chosen which explicitly speaks of marriage.[3] After the proclamation of the Gospel, the priest is to give a homily based on the sacred text, speaking about "the mystery of Christian marriage, the dignity of wedded love, the grace of the sacrament, and the responsibilities of married people, keeping in mind the circumstances of this particular marriage" (no. 57).

The celebration then proceeds with the rite of marriage proper. First, the priest addresses the couple with a formula provided in the ritual or with similar words (no. 59). The questions before the consent follow, asking the couple about their freedom of choice, fidelity to each other, and, if appropriate, the acceptance and education of children (no. 60). The exchange of consent by the couple is made by reciting a formula or answering the questions of the priest, with their right hands joined (nos. 61–3). The priest receives their consent by pronouncing a formula offered in the ritual (no. 64). After the exchange of consent and the reception of it by the priest, it is suggested that an acclamation of praise to God *(ad Dei laudem)* be made by the assembly (no. 65).[4] The explanatory rites of the blessing and exchange of rings are done at this time. The priest, using one of the formulas given in the ritual, blesses the rings,[5] then gives the rings to the bride and groom. The exchange of rings is done while reciting a formula prescribed by the ritual. The ritual suggests that after the exchange of rings the whole community sings a hymn or song of praise (no. 68).[6] The general intercessions come after the song of praise which may be followed by the profession of faith, if the rubrics of the day require it (no. 69).

---

[3] The Rite in Chapter I proposes three readings: Gen 1:26-28a, 31a; Eph 5:2a, 25-32; and Matt 19:3-6, but alternative texts are provided in Chapter V (nos. 179–222). Those texts which explicitly refer to marriage have been marked by an asterisk.

[4] The second typical edition offers an alternative text for the reception of consent which is not found in the first edition (no. 64).

[5] Paragraph 66 says that it is also possible to sprinkle the rings with holy water.

[6] This is another modification to the rite.

The Liturgy of the Eucharist proceeds as in the ordinary with the opportunity given to the bride and groom of bringing the eucharistic gifts to the altar. For the Eucharistic Prayer, any of the special prefaces for Marriage (nos. 234–6) is taken, as well as the special interpolations for Eucharistic Prayers I–III (nos. 71, 237–9). After the Lord's Prayer, the priest omits the embolism "Deliver us, Lord" and pronounces the Nuptial Blessing over the bride and groom.[7] The rite considers it an important element because it indicates that it "should never be omitted" (no. 72). At the end of the blessing prayer, the priest, omitting the prayer "Lord Jesus Christ," proceeds to the rite of giving the Sign of Peace (no. 75). Communion follows. The ritual indicates that communion under both species can be extended to the parents, witnesses, relatives, and friends of the bride and groom (no. 76).[8]

At the concluding rite, the priest gives the solemn blessing, adopting one of the formulas made available in the ritual (nos. 77, 249–50). And when the celebration of the Mass is completed, the witnesses and the priest sign the Marriage Record either in the sacristy or in the presence of the people, but never on the altar (no. 78).[9]

TEXTS AND SYMBOLS FOR THE INTRODUCTORY RITE

The Reception of the Couple

The new rite proposes two ways of receiving the couple at the beginning of the marriage liturgy in the church. The first option (nos. 45–7) is a reception at the door of the church where, vested for Mass, the priest, together with the other ministers, goes to meet the couple. He greets them in a friendly manner, showing that the Church shares in their joy. While the opening song is sung, the procession to the altar takes place with the ministers going first, followed by the priest and the couple. According to local custom, they may be accompanied at least by their parents and the two witnesses to their designated places. In the alternative form (nos. 48–50) the priest, vested for Mass, greets the couple at their designated places in the church building.

---

[7] The new typical edition, in contrast to the first, now gives musical notes for the Nuptial Blessing. Singing or chanting the Nuptial Blessing certainly intensifies the importance of this prayer and adds solemnity to the celebration.

[8] The Latin word used, *propinqui,* is vague and could be extended to include all in the wedding party.

[9] This signing of the register in the church is another innovation introduced by the revised ritual.

The first option, the reception at the door and the ensuing procession, symbolizes that the couple are the real ministers of the sacramental celebration. As Gerard Lukken comments, "by crossing the threshold of the church building and by solemnly walking in procession towards the altar, the bridal couple is equipped with an official, public and ordained 'being able to do.' In a non-verbal way the bridal couple is being installed as protagonists of the celebration."[10]

The Formulas

Two new formulas are proposed for the opening exhortation after the greeting. The first is addressed to the whole liturgical assembly, inviting everyone to accompany and support the couple, not only with prayers but also with their affection and friendship (no. 52). It makes reference to the intention of the couple to establish a new family and home and thus expresses the meaning which the rite gives to marriage. The second formula is addressed to the spouses. The priest, speaking on behalf of the Church community, welcomes the spouses and lets them know that the community shares in their joy. His words speak of marriage as "a total partnership of life" between the two (no. 53). The priest refers to this day as one of joy and gladness and conveys the community's wish that God would listen to them, watch over them, and send them God's help from heaven, and that God would grant all their petitions.

This introductory rite effectively presents a theology of marriage. It is a liturgical act, done before the assembly of the Church, with appointed witnesses, of whom the primary one is the officially designated priest. As a liturgical act, in which the couple are themselves the ministers, it indicates entry into a covenantal union, a union which is described as a complete partnership of life. As a married couple, the pair will constitute a distinctive household, in which the partnership is oriented to the creation of a family.

TEXTS AND SYMBOLS OF THE RITE OF THE MARRIAGE SACRAMENT

The celebration of the rites that constitute the sacrament of marriage takes place after the Liturgy of the Word and before the Eucharistic Liturgy. Here we examine the texts and symbols of that rite.

[10] Gerard Lukken, "Relevance of Semiotic Analysis to the Liturgical Sciences Illustrated in the Light of the Rite of Marriage," *Per Visibilia ad Invisibilia,* ed. Louis van Tongeren and Charles Caspers (Kampen: Kok Pharos Publishing, 1994) 303.

THE SCRUTINY

The Marriage Rite, properly speaking, begins with the scrutiny, an element which already appeared in the 1969 edition. According to P. M. Gy, the scrutiny, which was adopted from the German marriage ritual, is not a sort of pre-consent, nor is it intended to replace the preparatory inquiry that should have been made before the wedding itself.[11] Its role is to proclaim to the community the conditions which make a true marriage, conditions which the said inquiry should have already verified. The texts of the questions closely resemble the German ritual, although the third has been modified to be in accord with the sense of Vatican II's teaching on the responsibility of parents regarding the procreation and education of children.

The scrutiny starts off with an opening exhortation or address to the couple, which reads as follows in a translation from the original Latin (no. 59):

"Dearly beloved, you have come together into this house of the Church, so that before the minister of the Church and the community, your will to contract marriage may be fortified by the Lord with a sacred seal. Christ abundantly blesses your conjugal love; those whom he has already consecrated in baptism, he enriches and strengthens by a special sacrament, so that they may live in mutual and lasting fidelity and assume the other duties of Matrimony. Wherefore, in the presence of the Church, I ask about your intention."

This address mentions all the salient aspects of Christian marriage. It is a sacrament with sacramental character grounded in the sacrament of baptism. It signifies the enduring blessing of God, who already consecrated the two persons to himself in baptism and now strengthens them with another sacrament at this significant moment of their lives, when they enter the marriage union. As a sacrament, this is an ecclesial act, done in the presence of the community and the Church's designated witness. The ensuing sacramental union is one of mutual love and fidelity between the two. As such, it has to integrate other marital duties, such as giving life and education to children.

---

[11] The third question reflects the conciliar teaching expressed in GS 50. See Pierre-Marie Gy, "Le nouveau rituel romain du mariage," *La Maison-Dieu* 99 (1969) 131. Gy makes reference to the German ritual of 1950.

The same formula is repeated in the Rite of Marriage Outside the Mass (no. 93). In the Marriage Rite Between a Catholic Party and a Catechumen or a Non-Christian (no. 158), the reference to baptism has been omitted. A few changes have also been made to this formula in the Celebration of Marriage Assisted by a Layperson in order to express the fact that this person is acting in virtue of a delegation given by the bishop (no. 127).

The language of contract, omitted in the rite of 1969, is reintroduced in the 1991 formula. Apparently the reference to love in the rite of 1969 was found too vague, and experience suggested the need to reiterate the conjugal and contractual aspects of this love. The interrogations that follow take up the language of covenant. Hence, between the address and the interrogations the four elements of sacrament, love, contract, and covenant are intertwined in the description of Christian marriage.

All three questions (nos. 60, 94, 128, 159) have been adopted completely from the 1969 typical edition (no. 24), with just a few rubrical alterations. The first question inquires about their freedom of choice in entering matrimony, to guarantee that they have not been coerced or forced into this. The second concerns their resolve to cherish and honor each other for the rest of their lives. The third, which may be appropriately omitted for older couples, is an inquiry on the readiness of the couple to accept children lovingly as fruits of the marriage and gifts from God, as well as the responsibility to bring them up according to the law of Christ and the Church. These are not simply preliminary questions which serve to build up the exchange of consent. They reveal some elements of the Church's teaching on marriage itself; namely, that it is a partnership founded on the personal liberty of the parties; that it establishes a lifelong (hence, indissoluble) relationship characterized by mutual love and respect; and that it is ordained toward the procreation and education of children. These three questions, therefore, attempt to verify whether the couple accepts matrimony as the Church understands it.

EXCHANGE OF CONSENT

The exchange of consent is introduced by the priest's invitation, asking the couple to join their right hands and declare their intention to enter the marriage covenant before God in the presence of the gathered assembly (no. 61). Two forms are proposed, one of which was already given in the 1969 text. Both forms were based on Anglo-

Norman models.[12] The first is in the declarative form. The groom makes the declaration first, then the bride, using the same words. Each party expresses before God and the Christian community his or her acceptance of the partner and makes a solemn vow to remain faithful and true to him or her in good and bad times, in sickness and in good health, as well as promising to love and honor the other throughout his or her life (no. 62). This formula underlines fidelity to the marriage covenant and indissolubility of the marriage bond, key concepts in the Church's doctrine on marriage. Since consent, in Catholic teaching, is the essence of marriage, it is only proper that these two concepts are expressed in the formula used. The declarative form fits well with the theological view that considers the bride and bridegroom as the real ministers of the sacrament.

The alternative formula, in the traditional question and answer format, is given as an option which could be taken should pastoral necessity demand it.[13] This format was already in use in the Roman Ritual of 1614, although with a shorter and a slightly different wording.[14] In view of what we have already noted above concerning the significance of the declarative form, it is deemed suitable that the alternative form be used only in exceptional circumstances.[15]

[12] P. M. Gy maintains that the formula "I, N., take thee, N., to be my lawful wife, to have and to hold, from this day forward, for better, for worse, for richer, for poorer, in sickness and in health, till death do us part," from which the present formula is based, has been found in the following rituals: for the period before the Reformation, *Manuale ad usum percelebris Ecclesiae Sariburensis* (Salisbury), ed. A. J. Collins (London: Henry Bradshaw Society 91, 1960) 47–8, and *Manuale et processionale ad usum insignis Ecclesiae Eboracencis* (York), ed. Henderson (Durham: Surtees Society 63, 1875) 27 and 167; for the period after the Reformation, H. Thurston, *Our Catholic Marriage*, rev. ed. (London: n.p., 1948), among others. See Gy, "Le nouveau rituel romain," 132, n. 19. This claim is confirmed by Kenneth Stevenson, *To Join Together: The Rite of Marriage* (New York: Pueblo Publishing, 1987) 139.

[13] The priest addresses the question to the groom first and then to the bride. Each of the spouses is to respond, "I do" (no. 63).

[14] For the exchange of consent in the 1614 Ritual, the priest asks each of the spouses whether they accept the other as a legitimate husband or wife, according to the rite of the Holy Mother the Church, to which each is to respond, *"Volo"* ("I do"). See *Rituale Romanum*, Tit. VII, cap. 2.

[15] Such as when one or both spouses cannot or find it difficult to read or write.

For the reception of consent the new rite gives two formulas. The first has been taken over from the 1969 edition, while the second is a new formulation. The former is a development from the formula of the post-Tridentine revision. It reads: "May the Lord kindly confirm the consent you have manifested before the Church, and fill you with his blessings. Let no man separate what God has joined."

While the revised texts of 1969 and 1991 have kept the Tridentine practice of having the priest demand and receive the consent of the spouses, they have also modified the formula. To manifest more clearly the role of the spouses as the main protagonists and the secondary role of the priest, the active *"Ego coniungo"* ("I join you") has been substituted by a formula which indicates that it is not the priest but the Lord who joins them in marriage, in virtue of their own mutual consent. The ecclesial dimension of the sacrament of marriage is highlighted by the presence of an assembled community to witness together what has been done. The formula has also been enriched biblically with the inclusion of the well-known Gospel verse on the indissolubility of Christian marriage (Matt 19:6; Mark 10:9).

The alternative text reads: "May the God of Abraham, the God of Isaac, the God of Jacob, the God who joined the first couple together in paradise, confirm and bless in Christ, this consent which you have manifested before the Church. May no one separate what God has conjoined" (no. 64). It is likewise biblically inspired, borrowed from an ancient bridal blessing formula pronounced by the priest at the end of the Mass of the veiling, before the newlyweds left the church.[16] It uses a biblical form of naming God, that is, as "God of Abraham, God of Isaac, God of Jacob," which has been traditional in marriage rites. It traces marriage back to the beginning of creation, with God as author. It is the same God who confirms and blesses marriage in and through Christ. What is thus accentuated here is the relationship of marriage with the history of salvation. Like the first formula, it ends with the Gospel injunction on the indissolubility of marriage.

---

[16] The Commentary on the 1991 Ritual by the Sacred Congregation on Divine Worship makes reference to Edmond Marténe, *Ordo III: Ex ms. Pontificali monasterii Lyrensis, annorum 600*, in *De antiquis Ecclesiae ritibus*, 1. I, c. IX, art. V, as the source of this prayer. See *Notitiae* 26 (1991) 315; Adrien Nocent, "Il matrimonio cristiano," *Anamnesis: Introduzione storico-teologica alla liturgia* Vol. 3:1 (Rome: Marietti, 1986) 348–50.

After the exchange of consent, the marriage order prescribes a brief acclamation of praise. This element appears for the first time in the official Roman Rite of Marriage.[17] The formula suggested has the priest invite the assembly to praise God, the congregation responding, "Thanks be to God." Other acclamations, however, may be used. Without a doubt, this acclamation enables the assembly to have greater participation in the liturgical celebration. It is the community's way of acknowledging that marriage is primarily the work of God, that this marriage has been in God's plan, and that the marriage relationship will never succeed apart from God's grace and help. It is then a recognition of the fact that the assembled community is a "co-destinator and as such also co-verifier of the event."[18]

BLESSING AND GIVING OF RINGS

In essence this is an explanatory rite. It has the purpose of reinforcing and intensifying the central rite which is the exchange of consent. It should never be seen, therefore, as though it were a rite separate from it. Nor should it be allowed to overshadow or to eclipse it.

The Blessing of the Rings

The three formulas provided for the blessing of rings have been completely taken over from the 1969 order. The first of these, which is the sample text given in the various rites (nos. 66, 100, 134, 165), is a simple invocation over the rings: "May the Lord bless + these rings which you give to each other as a sign of your love and fidelity." It is based on a twelfth-century rite from Rennes, Normandy.[19] This short prayer expresses directly the symbolic meaning of the ring in marriage. As a prayer of benediction, it intensifies the solemnity of the exchange. The commitment to love and fidelity does not concern the spouses alone. God blesses the union signified, and the hand of God is present in the continuance of love and fidelity between the spouses.

The second formula (no. 229) is a traditional blessing prayer from the Roman Ritual, already attested to around the tenth through eleventh centuries in the benedictional of Robert, archbishop of

---

[17] This acclamation after the exchange of consent, however, already appeared in the Spanish Matrimonial Ritual of 1966. See Dionisio Garcia Borobio, *Inculturación del matrimonio. Ritos y custombres matrimoniales de ayer y hoy* (Madrid: San Pablo, 1993) 147–8.

[18] Lukken, "Relevance of Semiotic Analysis," 308.

[19] Stevenson, *To Join Together,* 140.

Rouen.[20] It is quite interesting to see how this old prayer has been revised. It reads: "Lord, bless these rings, which we bless + in your name; that those who wear them may keep complete fidelity to each other, may remain in peace and in your goodwill and always live together in love. Through Christ."

There are modifications in this text from the Roman Ritual of 1614. There is no introductory dialogue. To avoid unnecessary duplication, only one gesture of blessing (out of the two in the 1614 ritual) has been preserved. In reference to the ring(s) and the user(s), there is a shift from the singular to the plural. This can be explained by the fact that in the 1614 ritual, mention is made of one ring only, that given by the groom to the bride. The new text avoids the suggestion of inequality between the bride and groom. The exchange of rings underscores the equality of bride and groom and the mutual character of the relationship in which the partners take equal initiative. In the prayer, the symbolism of the rings as tokens of fidelity and love is stressed. It expresses as well the longing that they remain in God's peace and goodwill.

The third formula (no. 230) was composed for the 1969 ordo and reads as a blessing of the spouses rather than of the rings, thus expressing a theological preference to bless people rather than objects. The prayer, first of all, implores God to bless and consecrate the spouses in their love. It then moves on to entreat the Lord to make the rings symbols of the spouses' faith and reminders of their mutual love. The faith, no doubt, is faith in each other, but more deeply, it is faith in God's action in the sacrament of marriage.

The Exchange of Rings (nos. 67, 101, 135, 167)

The exchange of rings follows the blessing. Accompanying the gesture of putting the ring on the finger of the partner is a formula to be recited by each of the spouses. "N., accept this ring as a sign of my love and fidelity. In the name of the Father, and of the Son, and of the Holy Spirit." This is a formula based on one of the earliest marriage texts known to us. It is from the marriage of Judith, daughter of Charles the Bald, to Edilwulf, King of East Anglia in 856 C.E.[21] It ex-

---

[20] Korbinian Ritzer, *Formen, riten und religiöses Brachtum der Eheschliessung in den christlichen Kirchen des estern Jahrtausends,* Liturgiewissenschaftliche Quellen und Forschungen 38 (Münster: Aschendorf, 1962) 363. Quoted in Gy, "Le nouveau rituel romain," 135.

[21] See Ritzer, *Formen, riten und religiöses Brachtum,* 258–60. Quoted in Stevenson, *To Join Together,* 140.

presses the symbolic meaning of the ring in marriage quite simply, while calling, as it were, on the Holy Trinity to seal and consecrate the bond. It is notable that the spouses take turns in pronouncing the formula, in contrast to the 1614 ritual where the priest did almost all the talking. The transformation, therefore, signals also a change in understanding of the nature of marriage; namely, that it is an action of the couple and it is reciprocal.

THE SONG OF PRAISE

An element not found in the 1969 edition, the possibility of singing a hymn or a song of praise after the exchange of rings, is a welcome addition to the rite (nos. 68, 102, 136, and 168). Aside from the fact that it is another occasion on which the participation of the community is guaranteed, the joy of the moment also demands it. The community, as "co-destinator" and "co-verifier," has to have a means to express its joy in the couple's exchange of consent, as well as its affirmation and support of this important existential decision they have just manifested.

The Symbols

Having examined the formulas of the marriage rite proper, let us now give more attention to the symbols and gestures which they accompany.

THE JOINING OF HANDS

This ancient symbolic gesture of joining the hands of the spouses was originally carried out by the father or guardian of the bride. It signified the "handing over" of the bride to the groom who has "requested for the hand" of the woman. Beginning with the eighth century, however, the priest takes over the task from the father or guardian.[22] In other places, this was accompanied by the rite in which the priest placed the stole in the form of a cross or wrapped it around the joined hands of the couple. He did this while pronouncing a blessing which, at first, was simply the Trinitarian formula.[23] Later on,

[22] The Ritual of Meaux describes that the priest joins the hands of the spouses with the accompanying words, *Ego trado N. tibi in uxorem.* See Borobio, *Inculturación del matrimonio,* 28.

[23] J. B. Molin, "Symboles, rites et textes du mariage au Moyen Age Latin," *La celebrazione cristiana del matrimonio,* ed. G. Farnedi, 107–27, Studia Anselmiana 93; Analecta 11 (Rome: Pontificio Ateneo S. Anselmo, 1986). Quoted in Borobio, *Inculturación del matrimonio,* 28.

however, the formula became *Ego coniungo vos . . .* , which was then adopted by the Roman Ritual of 1614.

The joining of the right hands at the moment of the exchange of consent (nos. 61, 95, 129, and 160) is a nonverbal proclamation of the couple's intention to enter into the marital union. It is a fitting gesture that accompanies the declaration of their consent or resolve to take and accept each other as husband and wife all the days of their lives. One could argue that this symbolic action has the substance of a manifesto concerning the permanency and indissoluble quality of the marriage relationship. It serves to reinforce the reciprocal nature of the marital relationship, of the equality that exists between bride and groom, between husband and wife. The injunction designating the right hand rather than left seems to underscore the fact that this action has the character of a solemn oath or pledge, just as people normally raise their right hands when taking oaths. Also, this action reinforces the spouses' public declaration of exclusive reciprocity. "Within this circle of the *iunctio manuum*, the husband and wife promise each other exclusive faithfulness (cf. 'My wife,' 'my husband') in all circumstances."[24]

THE GIVING OF RINGS

The ritual action of the giving of rings in marriage originated as an element in a rite of betrothal or engagement, where it was a sign or symbol of the commitment to marry in the future. In the East, this still remains the core of the betrothal rites.[25] In the West, however, it has become an explanatory rite in the marriage rite proper. Isidore of Seville, writing at the beginning of the seventh century, gives an explanation to this Roman custom:

"The fact that the man gives his fiancée a ring means that it is a sign of mutual faithfulness or, rather, that their hearts are bound by a single pledge. Hence it is placed on the fourth finger, for in that finger, it is said, there is a vein which carries the blood to the heart. In ancient times, a woman could not be given in marriage more than once, lest her love be divided among more than one husband."[26]

[24] Lukken, "Relevance of Semiotic Analysis," 309.

[25] For a short review of the historical development of this rite, see Stevenson, *To Join Together,* esp. pp. 3–83.

[26] Isidore of Seville, *De ecclesiasticis officiis* 2.20.5-8. In Migne, *Patrologia latina* 83.810c-812b. English translation in Mark Searle and Kenneth Stevenson, *Documents of the Marriage Liturgy* (Collegeville: The Liturgical Press, 1992) 119.

This sense of the rite is still valid today, where the practice is preserved. Popular interpretations often refer to the round-shape of the ring which signifies eternity. As a circle does not have any beginning or ending, so the commitment of the spouses is undying. The ring is a token of love and fidelity. Handing it over to the beloved constitutes a promise of exclusivity; it is a ritual gesture that manifests absolute, complete self-giving to the spouse.

Throughout the history of the marriage rite, different forms of carrying out the rite have been noted. As noted above, in the ritual of 1614 only one ring is mentioned. It is first blessed and sprinkled with holy water by the priest; then he hands it over to the groom who, in turn, places it on the ring finger of the bride while the priest recites the Trinitarian formula, making the sign of the cross over them. In the present rite two rings are used, allowing an exchange between the couple. In the 1614 ritual, the ring which the groom presented to the bride was received by her as a symbol of her integral fidelity, a pledge of her noble love for her husband. The present rite does not speak of a "handing-over" of the ring but of the "exchange of rings" to highlight reciprocity and mutual responsibility in preserving the unity of marriage.

The joining of hands, the exchange of rings, and the rings themselves are of no little consequence in Christian marriage. They are symbols or symbolic gestures which manifest that marriage is a relationship grounded on the spouses' mutual consent and acceptance as husband and wife until death. They express the exclusive and indissoluble character of Christian marriage entered into by the partners out of their individual initiative. The symbolic actions likewise underline the equality of the spouses in the marital union.

ADDITIONS TO THE ORDER

Some additional rites in the new order deserve our attention.

Marriage Rite Presided by a Lay Officiant

BACKGROUND

Appearing for the first time in the Roman ritual for marriage, this rite responds to the disposition of canon 1112 of CIC 1983, which prescribes that "with the prior favorable opinion of the conference of bishops and after the permission of the Holy See has been obtained, the diocesan bishop can delegate lay persons to assist at marriages where priests or deacons are lacking."[27] This provision is also a novelty in the code and was inspired by the Instruction *Sacramentalem indolem* of the Congregation for the Discipline of the Sacraments of May 15, 1974,[28] in which diocesan bishops were granted the faculty to grant laypersons the exercise of the function of qualified witness of the Church in the celebration of marriage. The concession allows this witness, therefore, to ask for and receive the consent of the spouses on behalf of the Church (can. 1108, § 2).[29] The conditions to be fulfilled before such a capacity is granted are laid down in the said canon and repeated in number 25 of the introduction to the order. In regard to the choice of the layperson, however, paragraph 2 of canon 1112 specifies that "a suitable lay person should be chosen who is capable of giving instructions to those to be wed and qualified to perform the marriage liturgy correctly." Moreover, such a delegated layperson is responsible for all the canonical as well as civil formalities of the marriage (can. 1121–3).

Suffice it to say that the introduction of this rite is truly an enrichment, a landmark in the development of the marriage ritual. It is one which truly responds to the pastoral situation not only in missionary areas but also in developed countries where the scarcity of ordained ministers is a real problem.

TEXTS FOR THE RITE

In terms of structure and contents, this celebration is essentially similar to the rites in which the ordained preside, particularly the celebration of marriage outside Mass. There are, nevertheless, guidelines which specify the place the lay officiant must occupy, the vesture to be worn, and the attitude to be adopted in order to clearly distinguish this role from the liturgical presidency proper to the ordained.[30] Some texts have also been modified in order to express more explic-

[27] CIC, can. 1112, §1. It is not absolutely clear whether female laypersons may also receive this delegation or faculty, but it may be assumed, given the prevailing Latin usage that employs the masculine for the collective.

[28] Text can be found in Reiner Kaczynski, *Enchiridion Documentorum Instaurationis Liturgicae* 2 (Rome: Marietti, 1988) 50–2 (nos. 3306–8).

[29] Julian Lopez, "La segunda edición del ritual del matrimonio. Aspectos teológicos y pastorales," *Phase* 203 (1994) 414.

[30] The text of 1991, no. 25, uses the word *laicos,* which is masculine but can be inclusive. In some countries the faculty is in fact given to women as well as to men.

itly that the layperson is acting in an official capacity as a witness of the Church.

The formula for opening the celebration has been taken from the Book of Blessings.[31] Instead of the usual formulas and gestures used by the priest or deacon, the layperson blesses God by saying, "Blessed be God, the Father of all consolation, who has shown us his great mercy," to which the congregation responds, "Amen" or "Blessed be God forever" or some other reply. The formula for announcing the proclamation of the Gospel has been influenced by the Benedictionale.[32] The same can be said of the concluding blessing, which is manifestly distinct from the customary or ordinary blessing given by a priest. The text directs the lay presider to conclude the rite by making the sign of the cross while saying the following formulary:

"May God fill us with joy and hope in believing.
May the peace of Christ exult in our hearts
May the Holy Spirit lavish his gifts upon us."

It is, however, the text of the exhortation or address to the couple before the consent which puts in bold relief the lay presider's status as an official delegate of the Church:

"My dear N. and N., you have come here together, so that your will to contract marriage before me, who has been delegated by our bishop to assist at it, and before the community of the Church, may be fortified by the Lord by a sacred seal" (no. 150).

The nuptial blessing for this rite displays some peculiarities, in contrast to the other formulas suggested for use by an ordained minister. It appears for the first time in the 1991 ritual (nos. 139–40). What marks it off from the ordinary texts of the nuptial blessing is its responsorial structure; namely, after each of the three exclamations of praise addressed to the Persons of the Trinity the congregation responds with "Blessed be God." Moreover, the rubric prefixed to the text specifies that the lay presider is to pronounce the prayer with joined, rather than extended hands, and exhort the participation of

[31] See no. 119 of the Book of Blessings under the section, "Blessing of Married Couple Outside Mass." See *De Benedictionibus, Rituale Romanum ex decreto sacrosancti Œcumenici Concilii Vaticani II instauratum auctoritate Ioannis Pauli II promulgatum. Editio typica* (Urbs Vaticana: Typis Polyglottis Vaticanis, 1985) 49.

[32] Instead of the usual "A reading from the holy gospel according to . . . ," the text in the new order says "Brethren, listen to the words of the holy gospel according to . . . ."

all, that is, in the responses. Both of these changes differentiate this text from those to be used by the ordained. The lay presider can also administer communion to those present as it is done in the rite of marriage outside the Mass presided by a priest or a deacon.

This rite is a genuine response to a very real need, although it does not pretend to answer every situation. It is the responsibility of the local Churches to find out how the rite may be adapted to their particular circumstances.

Rite of Blessing an Engaged Couple

BACKGROUND

In one of the appendices of the revised typical edition (nos. 253–71), one finds an *Ordo Benedictionis Desponsatorum* ("Rite for the Blessing of Engaged Couples"). This rite has been adapted from the Book of Blessings (nos. 195–214).[33] It is examined here as an element in a possible continuous rite, going from betrothal to wedding.

In the introduction of the rite, mention is made of the rationale for introducing it[34] into the ritual by referring to the "responsibility of parents, an exercise of their own apostolate, of helping their children to prepare themselves for marriage" (217).[35]

It goes on to point out the special character of the betrothal of Christian couples, as an occasion for the families to celebrate it with prayer and a special rite, asking the Lord to bring to fulfillment what is auspiciously begun by the engagement.[36] It places the beginning of the relationship of the couple in the betrothal, and the consummation in the actual marriage. In other words, what seems to be a secular or civil rite is now formally being placed in the context of prayer and liturgy.

On the question of liturgical leadership, there are many possibilities envisioned. It suggests that one parent from the families of either side

[33] The official Latin text is found in *De Benedictionibus, Rituale Romanum ex decreto sacrosancti Œcumenici Concilii Vaticani II instauratum auctoritate Ioannis Pauli II promulgatum. Editio typica*, 79–84.

[34] Betrothal services did exist after Trent in some local rituals. See, for example, the Ritual of Coutances, given in Searle and Stevenson, *Documents of the Marriage Liturgy*, 190–4. This service, however, has more of the character of an inquiry and of a legal commitment than that of a liturgical ceremony.

[35] Order, no. 253a.

[36] No. 253b.

presides. However, in case a priest or a deacon is present, the office of presiding is to be given to him. In this case, care must be taken that people not get confused. It must be made clear to all that the "blessing is not the celebration of the sacrament of marriage itself" *(dummodo perspicuum adstantibus evadat non agi de celebratione Matrimonii)*. Aside from priests, deacons, and parents of both families, the introduction also mentions other lay persons, presumably either officially delegated by the Church or some other respected relative of the families concerned.

As for the suitable time for celebrating this rite, it is envisaged primarily as a family celebration, when the families of both partners come together (ROCM 254). The introduction suggests that it may also be done "during the engagement period on an occasion when couples are brought together for premarital instruction."[37] It cautions, however, that this celebration should never be combined with the celebration of the Mass, for the same reason of avoiding confusion with the celebration of the sacrament of marriage itself.

STRUCTURE AND TEXTS

The rite begins with a greeting and brief introductory words to prepare the couple and everyone present. A liturgy of the word follows, composed of a scripture reading, responsorial psalm, and a brief homily or explanation of the reading. The intercessions and an exchange of rings or gifts come after the Liturgy of the Word. This is then followed by what is called the prayer of blessing *(oratio benedictionis)*, which is the principal euchological text of the liturgy. A short blessing of dismissal concludes the celebration. The celebration allows for more adaptations to various circumstances. Number 219 of the introduction states that "while maintaining the structure and chief elements of the rite, the minister should adapt the celebration to the circumstances of the place and the people involved."

Two formulas are proposed for the greeting, one for a priest or deacon and another for a lay presider. As in the Marriage Rite Celebrated Before a Lay Officiant, the distinction between ordained and non-ordained presiders is maintained. The introductory words supplied as a model explain the reason for the gathering, emphasizing Christians' need for God's grace at the time of engagement, as they prepare to form a family. The community is thus invited to pray for the engaged couple, particularly for their growth in mutual respect and love, as

[37] No. 256a.

well as for a suitable and chaste preparation for marriage through companionship and common prayer (no. 259).

For the Liturgy of the Word there are four texts given: John 15:9-12 (on the commandment of love); 1 Corinthians 13:4-13 (on the virtue of love); Hosea 2:21-26 (on the promise of fidelity); and Philippians 2:1-5 (on unity in spirit and ideals). It is worth noting that the three texts provided for the first reading are new introductions into the ritual. They are surely an enrichment to the lectionary for marriage. There is one text provided for the responsorial psalm (Psalm 145:8-9, 10 and 15:17-18) with the response, "The Lord is compassionate to all creatures." The rubric in number 264 gives the advice that when circumstances suggest it, a brief explanation of the Scripture text be given so the assembly may understand the meaning of the celebration and its difference from the celebration of marriage.

For the intercessions there is a provision that only those best suited for the occasion may be used. Likewise, other intentions that apply to the situation may be composed. The texts of the proposed intercessions are interesting in that the first part of the petition is a recalling of the Lord's deeds. The first four petitions concern what the Father has done, while the fifth recalls how Christ mystically prefigured the spousal love of the sacrament of marriage in his paschal sacrifice for his own spouse, the Church. The response to each invocation is, "Lord, help us to remain in your love." Following the intercessions is the signing of the pledge or the exchange of rings or other gifts. It is suggested that, "in accord with local custom, before the prayer of blessing, the engaged couple may express some sign of their pledge to each other, for instance, by signing a document or by exchanging rings or gifts" (no. 266). Before the rings or gifts are exchanged, however, they are to be blessed with the proposed or some other similar formulary.

Two formulas are provided for the prayer of blessing, one for use either by a lay presider, who must pronounce it with joined hands, or by a priest or deacon who prays with extended hands. The prayer thanks God for drawing the couple together, then asks the Lord to strengthen their hearts so that they may keep faith in each other, please God in all things, and so come auspiciously to the celebration of the sacrament (no. 268). The other formula is for the use of either a deacon or a priest. It locates the relationship of the couple in God's wise plan of providence and goes on to pray for the grace that, as they prepare for their marriage, they may grow in respect for one another and cherish one another with sincere love (no. 269).

The short rite is concluded with a brief blessing which resembles the formulas of the Prayers Over the People in the Sacramentary. It prays for the abiding presence of God in the lives of the couple so that the Lord might always guide their steps and strengthen their hearts in God's love.

The inclusion (or reintroduction) of this rite of blessing for engaged couples is, without doubt, very significant. It represents a recognition that indeed in some local Churches, the practice of celebrating a rite of engagement survives. There is an acknowledgment of the positive value that this custom or tradition has in view of Christian marriage. In fact, given the gradual loss of the religious character of marriage in contemporary society, familial rites such as this might be helpful in reversing the tide. It might be worth considering, however, making this rite a constitutive part of the rite of marriage itself, particularly in localities where marriage is celebrated in various stages. In such a celebration this rite of engagement could be looked upon as a first stage of a process which reaches its high point in the celebration in Church with the exchange of consent, and climaxes in the home for the wedding party.

CONCLUSION

The introduction and the essential rites of marriage in this newly revised order for the celebration of marriage offer both theological and liturgical principles for the celebration of marriage. These are principles which can serve as guides in the preparation and adaptation of marriage rituals by the local churches, even in the more radical way that is foreseen in the document's own principles of inculturation.

The key theological term to the understanding of the sacrament of marriage is covenant. The union between man and woman symbolizes the union between God and his people in covenant, and most especially the union between Christ and the Church. It is a covenant that owes its existence to God's gracious initiative, but it is grounded in the original act of creation, whereby God made man and woman one, pledged to one another in a lasting bond of unity, and as God's cooperators committed to the procreation and education of children within the social unit of the family. As signified at the wedding in Cana of Galilee, Christ raised this natural union to the dignity of sacrament under the new dispensation.

Entering into the sacrament of marriage, the couple acts in accordance with their original baptismal consecration, for marriage between Christians has a sacramentality that is rooted in their baptismal consecration. The revised order highlights, in several ways, the fact that it is the couple themselves who are the ministers of the sacrament, and it is their union which has sacramental significance. With this in mind, the ritual in its principles and in its ordering of rites brings out the ecclesial character of this sacramental celebration and union. The married couple takes up its place within the community of the Church, and is aided by this community in preparation for marriage, in its celebration, and in living in fidelity to the couple's marital commitments. These are commitments that include the mutual love and fidelity of husband and wife, the bearing and education of children in the faith, and witness to the Church of a union that mirrors or resembles that of Christ and the Church. The 1991 revision of the marriage rite theologically completes that of 1969 by giving due place to the role of the Holy Spirit in the call to marriage, in its preparation, in its celebration within the Church community, and in living out the marital bond.

Liturgically, the order lays down principles and guidelines that provide for a full and adequate sacramental celebration. Its first concern is to revise the essential parts of the ritual in such a way that the role of the couple is respected. It is they who, by free and mutual consent, enter into union and celebrate the sacrament as its ministers. It is, of course, important that this be done within the community of the Church, and before its officially designated officiant. Hence, the role of the priest (or lay presider, if this is the case) is properly expressed. Even in allowing considerable room for the inculturation of marriage rites, the order lays down that the consent must always be made before the Church's officially designated witness. To signify liturgically that this union is blessed by the Church and that the sacrament is a sacrament of the Church, it also prescribes that the nuptial blessing be retained in all revisions and adaptations of the rite.

While not every case allows it, the concern is that the celebration of marriage respect all the principles of a well-ordered liturgy to the fullest possible extent. To this end, it provides ample texts for a Liturgy of the Word. It also provides for the participation of the assembly, whether in chant or in prayer, or in showing its assent to the union forged between man and woman. The rite also follows the principle that all other sacraments be intimately related to the Eucharist, so that the preferred service is that of the celebration of marriage within Mass. Sacramental communion can be given under both kinds to the couple, and also to those who accompany them in this celebration. With its attention to the nuptial blessing and to such rites as the joining of hands or the exchange of rings, the text is marked by its sensitivity to the importance of symbolic actions and words. This same sensitivity is apparent in the principles for liturgical adaptation, where the order shows great openness to whatever may enhance the symbolism and significance of the marriage rite among different peoples, in keeping with their own distinctive cultural practices, customs, and beliefs.

Further concern for an adequate liturgy is shown in two particular provisions of this 1991 rite of marriage. The first is the ruling that in the absence of a priest or deacon, the designation of a lay person to preside at a wedding is possible. This is one way of assuring both the ecclesial nature of marriage and a properly celebrated liturgy. The second provision is found in the appendix which provides a rite of betrothal. Use of this rite would express the Church's concern for the couples as they begin their preparation for their wedding, and makes it possible to place the entire process of entering marriage in a liturgical framework.

These principles that guide the celebration of the sacrament of marriage provide the context for a more detailed examination of the celebration of the Word and of the prayer texts, or euchology, given in the revised rite.

Chapter III

The Celebration of the Word and Euchology

In this chapter we want to examine the texts proposed in the revised order for the celebration of the Word and for the euchological or prayer texts.

THE CELEBRATION OF THE WORD

The 1969 order of marriage ameliorated the scriptural poverty of the 1570 Roman Missal, which gave only two scriptural readings for the nuptial Mass.[1] Its lectionary provides thirty-five biblical passages: eight Old Testament readings, ten from the apostolic letters, and ten from the Gospels. For the psalmody seven texts were chosen, and for the verse before the gospel there are four short texts from the First Letter of John the apostle.

The order of 1991 adopts the Neovulgate as the norm for liturgical use of the Scriptures, according to the prescriptions of the Apostolic Constitution *Scripturam thesaurus*.[2] This meant a change in some of the titles given to the readings to express their liturgical purpose.[3] However, it preserved all the texts suggested in 1969 and has added five more: Proverbs 31:10-13, 19-20; Romans 15:1b-3a, 5-7, 13; Ephesians 4:1-6; Philippians 4:4-9; and Hebrews 13:1-4a, 5-6b.

While granting the possibility of having three readings, the new order instructs that at least one of these should be explicitly about marriage. To indicate this preference, an asterisk is placed before the

---

[1] The 1570 Missal has Paul's letter to the Ephesians 5:22-33 as the epistle and Matthew 19:1-6 as the gospel reading.

[2] *AAS* 71 (1979) 557-9.

[3] See Romano Cecolin, "Il Lezionario del nuovo 'Ordo Celebrandi Matrimonium': Alcune annotazioni di carattere biblico-liturgico," *Rivista Liturgica* 79 (1992) 639-41.

texts.[4] It also shows a respect for the traditional texts which are included within the rites for the celebration of marriage within Mass and the rite of blessing engaged couples.[5] However, substitutions for these are allowed.

Writing on the lectionary of the 1969 order, G. Boggio[6] suggested five principal marriage themes, taken from the General Introduction to the ritual, which might serve as a guide in choosing the readings and under which the lectionary texts may be arranged. These include: marriage as a sign of love between Christ and the Church, mutual help and mission in the Church, conjugal pact and mutual fidelity, undivided love and charity, and children as the crowning of conjugal life. Although it must be admitted that the biblical texts are infinitely richer than these themes present, it seems convenient to tentatively arrange them under these headings. The titles given to the readings in the order are helpful in indicating the purpose of choosing these texts for the marriage liturgy.

Marriage as Sign of Love between Christ and the Church

The texts placed by Boggio under this heading are Revelation 19:1, 5-9; Ephesians 5:2, 21-33; and John 2:1-11. For Revelation 19, the title in the order relates marriage to the wedding feast of the Lamb in the heavenly Jerusalem and thus points to the sacrament's figurative and eschatological significance.

The title given to Ephesians 5:2, 21-33 relates the sacrament of marriage to the mystery of the union between Christ and the Church. Since the letter makes some use of the household codes of the time in describing relations between man and wife, the text has to be used carefully in today's social settings. In giving a title to John 2:1-11, the

[4] Of the forty-four texts suggested for use in the rite, thirteen have been marked with an asterisk. These include Gen 1:26-28, 31a; 2:18-24; 24:48-51, 58-67; Tob 7:6-14; 8:4b-8; Prov 31:10-13, 19-20, 30-31; Sir 26:1-4, 16-21; Eph 5:2a, 21-33; 1 Pet 3:1-9; Ps 127 (128):1-2, 3, 4-5; Matt 19:3-6; Mark 10:6-9; and John 2:1-11.

[5] For the celebration of marriage within Mass, the following readings are suggested: Gen 1:26-28; Ps 127 (128):1-2, 3, 4-5ac; Eph 5:2a, 25-32; and Matt 19:3-6. All of these are found in the lectionary for marriage, marked with an asterisk. In the rite of betrothal, five texts are proposed: John 15:9-12; 1 Cor 13:4-13; Hos 2:21-26; Phil 2:1-5; and Ps 144 (145):8, 9, 10. Only the text from John's Gospel and Psalm 144 are found in the lectionary. A brief commentary on these is presented in Cecolin, "Il Lezionario del nuovo," 644–9.

[6] Giovanni Boggio, "Temi biblici nel lezionario del matrimonio," *Rivista Liturgica* 63 (1976) 529–51.

account of the wedding feast at Cana, the order underscores Christ's presence and action at the wedding of Cana as a messianic sign.

Mutual Help and Mission in the Church

Another set of texts is related by Boggio to the role and mission of married couples in the Church, underlining thereby the ecclesial quality of this Christian sacrament.

The title given by the order to Genesis 2:18-24 underlines the union of man and woman in one flesh. Tobit 8:4b-8 tells of the beautiful prayer of Tobiah and Sarah on their first night together. The lectionary title picks out the phrase "we shall grow old together" to emphasize the lasting fidelity of the marriage union, which in Christian times has always been one of its essential properties. The text itself points to the divine assistance whereby such fidelity is made possible.

For Sirach 26:1-4, 16-21 (13-16), the title points to the enumeration of the qualities desired in a wife. Although the text has a lovely poetic style, the relation it suggests between husband and wife might be considered offensive to the sensibilities of the contemporary woman. Proverbs 31:10-13, 19-20, 30-31 is one of the new texts introduced in the 1991 revision of the order for marriage. As the lectionary title indicates, it too describes the virtues of the good wife and presents the same difficulties today as the reading from Sirach.

Romans 12:1-2, 9-18 speaks of the nature of New Testament worship, which is a life lived in obedience to the Gospel. The lectionary title shows that the text is applied to marriage by reason of its reference to the worship given in the body. The offering of the body to God in a spiritual sacrifice is realized in marriage with the offering which the couple together make of themselves to God.

Romans 15:1b-3a, 5-7, 13 was also introduced into the selection of readings by the 1991 revision. It is a selection of verses from this chapter of the epistle in which Paul exhorts the readers to treat each other in the community in ways exemplified by Christ. The title applies this Christ-like mutual behavior to the relations between wife and husband.

Ephesians 4:1-6 is another addition from 1991. In this text the author of the epistle exhorts the faithful to keep the unity of the Spirit and of the Body of the Church through a unity in love. The title given in the order highlights the unity which the letter extols, and gives this as a model to the bridal couple, both for their own life together and for their part in the life of the Church. The text could also be placed with those here included under the heading of undivided love and charity.

In 1 Peter 3:1-9 the writer gives practical advice for the married: to be like-minded, sympathetic, loving toward one another, kindly disposed, and humble. Since the writer relies on household codes of the time, the exhortation needs adaptation. The title given underlines the unity of the spouses in like-mindedness and their service in love to the fellowship of the Church.

From Matthew 5:13-16 on discipleship, the lectionary title has chosen the words "you are the light of the world," no doubt to bring out the public testimony given by a married couple to the kingdom of God.

Conjugal Pact and Mutual Fidelity

Boggio includes a number of readings under this thematic heading.

The verses of Tobit 7:6-14 are the blessing given to Jewish couples at the time of the narrative and the title in the lectionary points to this. Jeremiah 31:31-32; 32:33-34 describes the new covenant between God and the house of Israel and of Judah in uniting them as one, which is to be taken as an archetype of matrimony. However lovely these texts may be, they present difficulties in adapting their view of marital relationships to our present context where the relationship between man and woman is not the same as it was in that time.

Some texts have a moral purpose. The title given to Romans 8:31-35, 37-39 presents it as an assurance for couples concerning the solidity of the marriage bond that joins them together in Christ. It is Christ's love which allows them to weather all kinds of tests of their mutual love and covenant. In giving a title to 1 Corinthians 6:13-15, 17-20, a strong moral exhortation on Christian freedom, the marriage order picks out the verse, "your members are a temple of the Holy Spirit." Hebrews 13:1-4a, 5-6b was introduced in 1991 because it includes respect for marriage in presenting its ideals for Christian conduct.

Matthew 7:21, 24-29, for its part, underlines the necessity of building a life on the solid rock of God's Word.

Matthew 19:3-6 is the traditional text for marriage services in the West and accentuates Christ's affirmation of the indissolubility of marriage, already required in the order of creation according to the Genesis account. Mark 10:6-9 parallels Matthew 19:3-6. The titles given for both Matthew 19 and Mark 10 emphasize this indissoluble union.

Undivided Love and Charity

This is another thematic title chosen by Boggio to group certain readings. In presenting Genesis 24:48-51, 58-67, the story of the marriage of Isaac and Rebecca, the lectionary picks the verse which says that in her love for her husband Rebecca was consoled for the death of her mother. This is probably meant to suggest that the union of marriage is stronger than any other family relationship.

A few of the scriptural texts are about Christian love. The pericope on love from 1 Corinthians 12:31–13:8a applies to the married as it applies to all Christians, but it allows for a reflection on how love's qualities are realized in a Christian family. Colossians 3:12-17 is also a text about love as the bond of perfection. The reading from 1 John 4:7-12 shows how Christian love is but a share in God's own love, while 1 John 3:18-24 exhorts its readers to put love into action. Other texts on Christian love in the lectionary are Matthew 22:35-40; John 15:9-12; and John 15:12-16. All of these texts are capped by the selection from John 17:20-26, which presents the union of the persons in the Trinity as the model for communion among Christ's disciples.

Philippians 4:4-9 is a new text introduced in the 1991 revision. While it exhorts its readers to joy in the Lord, based on full trust in God, the title given to it denotes that it is the peace of heart given by God which makes constant trust, love, and joy possible.

The Children, Crowning of Conjugal Life

With a final thematic title, Boggio points to lectionary selections on the place of children in marriage.

Boggio relates Genesis 1:26-28, 31 to the fecundity of marriage, because of the command to increase and multiply in verse 22 which precedes the text. In this, he sees the likeness to God to which the text itself refers. His interpretation is somewhat forced, since it is the union as two in one flesh which the lectionary text underscores. It is in fact curious that while the prayer texts of the liturgy have much to say about fecundity, the lectionary selections give little attention to it.

Conclusion

Only a few of the texts offered in the revised order for the celebration of marriage have to do directly with marriage and as noted these are marked with an asterisk. Most of the passages proposed are applications to marriage of blessings or commands having to do with discipleship in general. The accommodation in some seems forced, but especially those which speak of Christian love are very suitable to marriage celebration.

Among the readings for the epistle of the liturgy, those which assume the prevailing household codes of their time stand out. These are Ephesians 5 and 1 Peter 3. Commentary on the text from Ephesians was important in the history of marriage in bringing to light its own sacramental character, and its relation to the covenant between Christ and the Church.[7] It can still serve that purpose, provided it is accompanied by good explanation as to the use of household codes. Another text that serves to bring out the sacramental significance of marriage is Revelation 19. While it may be hard to understand, its use of marriage imagery in describing the eternal blessedness of the Lamb of God and the heavenly liturgy is pertinent to the eschatological and sacramental meaning of marriage in Christ.

Besides being texts from among which to choose for the celebration of a marriage, these scriptural readings are helpful for a preparatory catechesis. Boggio's groupings help meet this purpose, as do the titles in the lectionary. However, nothing replaces the actual study of the text. Some texts that are inappropriate for the ceremony may serve a purpose in catechesis. Thus the reading from Tobit provides an occasion to discuss what is suitable in a marriage ritual and what blessings a couple might ask from God. The New Testament texts that incorporate household codes give examples of how early Christians tried to relate their vision of marriage to social expectations and moral norms. Today young couples have to face these issues, even though their responses will be quite different.

TEXTS FOR GENERAL INTERCESSIONS

The General Intercessions close the Liturgy of the Word. In Appendix I of ROCM two sets of formulas for General Intercessions are given. This is a welcome addition to the order of 1991. It is made clear that the texts given are only sample intercessions and thus it is safe to conclude that they may be adapted or that new intercessions may be composed.

The first set (no. 251) is made up of an invitatory prayer and a series of five petitions, three of which are for the newlyweds while the other two are for all of God's people and all married couples. What is asked of God for the couple are health of mind and body, fidelity to the covenant of marriage, fruitful and perfect love, mutual support and help, and witnessing to the gospel. The series of petitions is concluded by a brief prayer that the Spirit be poured out upon the spouses so that they may be one in mind and heart, that nothing would destroy their happiness, and that nothing put their union asunder.

[7] See Theodore Mackin, *The Marital Sacrament* (New York/Mahwah, N.J.: Paulist Press, 1989) 283–5.

48

The second formula (no. 252) gives five petitions of which only the first is directed toward the newlyweds. The rest are for their families and friends, all young people, families throughout the world and peace among nations, for relatives and friends, and for the Church. In the petition for the new couple what is asked is simply the future well-being of their family.

THE EUCHOLOGICAL OR PRAYER TEXTS

The prayer formulas of the marriage liturgy will be treated here in three parts. The first is an examination of the prayer texts for the nuptial Mass, which include the collects, prayers over the gifts, prefaces, interpolations for the Eucharistic Prayers, and post-communion prayers. An analysis of the texts of the nuptial blessing and the accompanying gestures will follow. The third part will study the texts of the blessings at the end of the Mass.

The Mass

In terms of euchological texts or prayer formulas for the Nuptial Mass, the new order provides an abundance compared to the post-Tridentine nuptial liturgy. The *Missa pro Sponsis* of the sixteenth-century Missal had some generic prayers which expressed beautiful ideas about the blessing of marriage and the propagation of the human race, but it said little of the sacrament of marriage. It did not have a proper preface for weddings.

Commenting on the euchological texts already given in the 1969 order, P. M. Gy notes that about one-third of its prayers and prefaces are ancient texts which were eventually touched up and recomposed. The other two-thirds are new creations.[8] He enumerates the central themes of the euchological prayers thus: the joy of the occasion, the marriage union and its place in the divine plan of salvation (1969 ritual, nos. 106, 109, 113, 114, and 122), love (nos. 107, 109, 114, and 123), the faith professed by the spouses in the sacrament, in which they will have to raise their children and to which they will witness (nos. 106, 108, and 123), and children, the fruits of the union (nos. 33, 108, 115, 118, 120, 121, 125; cf. 24c).[9] To this abundant selection of texts the 1991 text has added some more, which will be noted below.

[8] Marie-Pierre Gy, "Le nouveau rituel romain du mariage," *La Maison-Dieu* 99 (1969) 130. In note 15 he provides a list classifying the new and ancient texts. We are not going to provide the list now since the texts will be examined individually.

[9] Ibid., 129.

The rite of 1969 proposed four formulas for the Collect or Opening Prayer and the 1991 revision added two more. All the texts are found in numbers 223–8 of the ritual book.

The first collect is a prayer composed by using two sources from earlier times. The first part of the prayer has been adapted from a section in the nuptial blessing of the 1570 Roman Missal; the second part takes inspiration from the Collect of Wednesday within the Easter Octave.[10] The comparisons are made below, translating the text from the original Latin in both cases.

1570 Roman Missal Nuptial Blessing	Order of Marriage, no. 223
God, who has consecrated the conjugal *union (copula)* by such an excellent mystery that in the nuptial covenant it might stand forth as a sacrament of Christ and the Church . . . . Easter Collect	God, who has consecrated the conjugal *bond (vinculum)* by such an excellent mystery that in the nuptial covenant it might stand forth as a sacrament of Christ and the Church . . . .
. . . grant to your servants that in living out this sacrament in life they may hold what they perceived in faith. Through Christ our Lord.	. . . we ask you to give to your servants *that what they perceive in faith they may pursue in deed.* Through Christ our Lord.

Drawing on the nuptial blessing of the Roman Missal, the first part of this collect looks to the marriage union as a covenant and a sacrament of Christ and the Church. The petition of the prayer takes up an Easter collect in which it is asked that Christians might hold in their lives to the sacrament of the Easter mysteries which they looked to in faith in the Easter Vigil. The faith in the Easter mystery and its sacraments is transposed to the sacrament of marriage. It is asked that the couple, seeing it in faith as a sacrament of Christ and the Church, might live this out in deed.

The collect in number 225 of the order was composed for the 1969 ritual and develops the theme of conjugal unity and love: "Be present, Lord, to our supplications and graciously pour out your grace on

---

[10] Gy makes reference to P. Bruylants, *Les oraisons du missel romain* (Louvain: Mont César, 1952) n. 334, as his source. See Gy, "Le nouveau rituel," n. 15.

these your servants, so that joined together at your altars *(aped tua altaria)* they may be strengthened in mutual love."[11]

Another collect which first appeared in 1969 and retained in 1991 is that which is found in number 226 and translated here from the Latin of the order: "Grant, we ask, almighty God, that these your servants, to be joined in the sacrament of marriage, may grow in that which they profess in faith, and that they may enrich the Church with faithful offspring. Through . . . ."

This text places marriage in an ecclesial context. While praying for the couple who are going to be joined in the matrimonial sacrament, it asks not only that God may enable them to grow in the faith they publicly declare, but at the same time it entreats that through their children the Lord will enrich his Church.

The collect in number 224 is a good example of an editorial reworking. The text was originally a prayer over the gifts for the Nuptial Mass from the *Sacramentarium Fuldense*, a tenth-century book containing Visigothic material.[12] It has been emended in order to fit its new position and function as an opening prayer in the Nuptial Mass. The texts are shown in comparison and are translated from the original Latin:

Sacramentary of Fulda, 2608	Order of Marriage, no. 224
God who in creating the human race formed woman from man and united them in the unity of flesh, from that formation giving them a unity of sweetness, look propitiously on this votive sacrifice, and bind together in a bond of love those to be joined as a couple in conjugal covenant,	God, who in creating the human race willed unity between man and woman, bind together with a bond of love these your servants who are to be joined as a couple in conjugal covenant,
so that they may preserve mutual peace, never violate their conjugal covenant and bear fruit in charity, and keep them thus in your fear, so that you may multiply us also in your love. Through . . .	so that you may grant that they who are to bear fruit in charity may be witnesses of that same charity. Through . . .

---

[11] The text is translated directly from the Latin. The sacramentality of marriage as an act of worship is expressed in the reference to the altar of God.

[12] See Kenneth Stevenson, *To Join Together: The Rite of Marriage* (New York: Pueblo Publishing, 1987) 143. The Latin text may be found in K. Ritzer, *Formen,*

This retouched text develops with effectiveness the theme of nuptial love and covenant. It places marriage in the context of the divine plan, that is, the conjugal union has been willed by the Creator from the beginning, in creation. The idea of the formation of woman from man used in the Fulda Sacramentary, however, is omitted in the new collect in place of a more direct affirmation of unity or oneness. The reference to the offering of sacrifice appropriate to a prayer over the gifts is excluded in the collect. What is asked is stated more briefly than in the Fulda text; namely, that the couple remain together in unbreakable and fruitful love, becoming in their lives witnesses to the divine love which has joined them together.

The text in number 227 is an addition to the 1991 order. It is, however, an ancient prayer formulary taken from the Leonine or Verona Sacramentary (no. 1109).[13] The new edition proposes that this collect may also serve as an alternative to the nuptial blessing in case this is omitted in the celebration of marriage between a Catholic party and a catechumen or non-Christian (ch. IV, no. 174). There are no significant changes made to the old text, only minor grammatical corrections, so it is sufficient to give the text in English translation from the new ritual: "Listen, Lord, to our supplications and protect kindly what you have instituted for the increase of the human race, that those who have been joined by you the Creator may be preserved by your help. Through our Lord." The above prayer professes God's authorship of the marriage institution, harking back to the creation texts from the book of Genesis. It touches upon procreation as an end of marriage, willed by the Creator.

The other formulary for the collect introduced in 1991 (no. 228) was originally a part of the nuptial blessing in the Gelasian Sacramentary (no. 1450).[14] It was edited with all the necessary corrections for it to become a suitable opening prayer. It repeats the themes of God's intent in creation and of marital fecundity. Since no significant changes

Riten und Religiöses Brauchtum der Eheschliessung in den christlichen Kirchen des ersten Jahrtausend (Münster: Aschendorf, 1962), or in the French edition, *Le mariage dans les églises chrétiennes* (Paris: Les Éditions du Cerf, 1970) 447–8. It is from *Sacramentarium Fuldense Saeculi X*, ed. G. Richter and A. Schönfelder (Fulda: Abtei Fulda, 1912) n. 2608.

[13] See the "Commentarium" of the Sacred Congregation on Divine Worship in *Notitiae* 26 (1990) 323–4. Latin text can be found in Ritzer, *Le mariage*, 422.

[14] The Latin text is given in Ritzer, *Le mariage*, 426, and is from the edition by Mohlberg.

were made to the excerpt taken from the nuptial blessing, it is enough to give the English translation of the text in the new order:

"God, who from the beginning of the world's increase blessed it with the multiplication of offspring, look propitiously on our supplications and pour out the wealth of your blessings on your servants, so that joined together in mutual affection as conjugal partners, they may be united as a couple in likeness of mind and in mutual holiness. Through . . ."

Having examined the provenance and the themes presented by these formularies, it seems clear that they evidence a great improvement from the post-Tridentine ritual. There has been a retrieval and suitable editing of ancient texts so as to be in harmony with contemporary teaching on marriage. In content, each of these prayers develops or calls to mind one or another aspect of marriage, such as unity and fidelity among spouses, mutual love, conjugal union as part of the divine plan, indissolubility of the sacramental bond, Christian marriage as symbol of the love or covenant between Christ and the Church, joy brought about by this occasion, and procreation as an end of marriage. These are the themes noted in the introduction to the order of 1991.

PRAYERS OVER THE GIFTS

Three formulas (nos. 231, 232, 233) proposed for the prayers *super oblata* have been taken over from the 1969 edition. The first is a text from the 1570 Roman Missal *(Missa votiva pro sponsis)*, with a minor addition:[15] "Receive, Lord, the gift we offer for those joined in holy marriage and since you are the one who bestows the action, order it also according to your providence. Through . . ."

The second formula is a text composed for the 1969 revision of the order of marriage: "Kindly accept, O Lord, the gifts which we offer in joy and keep safe with your fatherly mercy those whom you have joined in the covenant of this sacrament."

Like number 232, the third formula is a text that was drawn up for the first typical edition of 1969. It shows the close link that exists between the sacrament of marriage and the Eucharist: "Look with mercy, Lord, upon our supplications and accept with serene countenance the gifts which we offer for these servants now joined as a

[15] See Stevenson, *To Join Together*, 144.

couple in holy covenant, so that these mysteries may be strengthened in their mutual charity and by your love. Through . . ."

These three formulas make clear the connection between the sacraments of Eucharist and marriage. There is the appreciation of Christ's love, which the Eucharist celebrates, as the model and source of the couple's capacity to love God and each other in total fidelity. It is for this reason that the Eucharist is "offered" for them. There is, likewise, the consciousness of God's authorship of marriage. The union of two persons in marriage has been in the divine plan from the beginning. Consequently, it looks upon God for its protection and success. Therefore, by virtue of its sacred character it is best described as a covenant (*foedus*), which is sealed by a sacrament.

POST-COMMUNION PRAYER TEXTS

The three texts found in numbers 245, 246, and 247 are a carry-over from the typical edition of 1969. The first is an emended version of the post-communion prayer in the 1570 Missal (Votive Mass for Weddings), with some material from the 1738 Parisian Missal on the power of the sacrifice offered. The phrase "that you may make them harmoniously one in charity" is probably an adaptation from the prayer after communion of Easter in the *Missale Romanum*.[16] The text reads in English translation: "Lord, by the power of this sacrifice, accompany with favor what in your providence you have instituted, that those whom you have joined in this holy partnership (and nourished with one bread and one cup), may indeed become harmoniously one in charity. Through . . ."

In this prayer the connection between marriage and Eucharist is made explicit. The Eucharist, as both sacrifice and sacrament, is a model and an efficacious symbol of the couple's union, their oneness of heart, in matrimony, for it is in the partaking of the one bread and the one cup that the marital union reaches its highpoint. There is also a shift in the language on marriage from the canonical to the more spiritual. While the 1570 Missal speaks of the couples as being joined together in a "legitimate partnership" (*legitima societate connectis*), the typical editions refer to a "holy partnership" (*sancta societate iunxisti*).

The second prayer (no. 246) was also composed for the 1969 typical edition. It relates participation in the sacrament of marriage to participation at the Lord's table. The Eucharist is looked upon as reinforcing

[16] Gy, "Le nouveau rituel," 130, especially n. 15.

and completing the marital bond in which the newlyweds have been joined. It adds an apostolic dimension to the life of the married by noting their proclamation of Christ's name through their very union as a couple. The text reads in translation: "Made partakers of your table, we ask you, Lord, that those who have been joined together by the sacrament of marriage may always adhere to you, so that they may announce your name to others. Through . . ."

The third formula (no. 247) was likewise composed for the 1969 order. It is filled with eucharistic overtones relating to both sacrament and sacrifice and reads as follows: "Grant, we ask you, Lord, that the power of the sacrament which they have received may increase in your servants, and that the effect of the host which we have offered may be received by all present. Through . . ."

The prayer connects Eucharist and marriage, asking that through the reception of the Eucharist the power of the sacrament of marriage may now increase. It also prays for the effect of the eucharistic sacrifice for all who have partaken in the service, thus adverting to the participation of the community.

What these three post-communion prayer formulas clearly highlight is the close connection between the two sacraments of marriage and Eucharist. The Eucharist does not only add solemnity to the celebration but is recognized as an efficacious symbol of the conjugal union. The marriage reaches its climax in the Eucharist. Like the other euchological prayers examined earlier, they point to the origin of marriage in God's will and plan, and its dependence on God for fruitfulness and success. Furthermore, in these prayers, the missionary dimension of the sacrament is intimated in the expectation that the bride and bridegroom, conjoined in matrimony, will witness to the love of the God which the Eucharist celebrates.

FORMULAS FOR THE PREFACE

Three preface texts are provided in numbers 234, 235, and 236, all of which were already present in the 1969 rite. In the 1991 revision, titles which specify the central themes of the texts have been added.[17]

---

[17] A careful study of the sources of these prefaces is given in Anthony Ward and Cuthbert Johnson, "The Sources of the Roman Missal (1975) II: Prefaces," *Notitiae* 23 (1987) 859–74. In this work the authors confirm Gy's conclusions in "Le nouveau rituel," 130, n. 15.

The first text is a slight reworking of an ancient Roman preface for the nuptial Mass.[18] The revised edition has given to this prayer the thematic title, "On the dignity of the marriage covenant." The text reads in translation:

"It is truly worthy and right, just and salutary, always and everywhere for us to give you thanks, Lord, holy Father, almighty and eternal God: Who have bound the covenant of marriage by a sweet yoke of harmony and an insoluble bond of peace, so that their chaste and fruitful holy marriage may multiply your adopted children. For it is by your providence and your grace, Lord, that you dispense in ineffable ways, both that generation may produce adornment to the world, and that regeneration may lead to the increase of the Church: through Christ our Lord. Through him, with the angels and all the saints, we sing to you without end our hymn of praise saying . . ."

The prayer describes marriage as a covenant of God's making. Because of its covenantal character, it is considered an unbreakable but sweet bond. The union is chaste due to the fidelity of the spouses to one another. The prayer, quite rightly, places marriage within an ecclesial framework when it points to the role of marriage in realizing the growth of the Church, the family of God's adopted children. The relationship between the sacraments of baptism and marriage is here brought into bolder relief. While the generation of children in marriage increases the family of humankind, their regeneration in baptism enlarges the family of God. The concluding part has been simplified in this edition, with the deletion of references to the whole array of heavenly powers. The revised text is content to refer only to the angels and all the saints. As usual in prefaces, the offering of praise through Jesus Christ powerfully and summarily expresses the conviction that it is only through the power of Christ and God's plan fulfilled in him that everything for which thanks is given in the prayer, especially for the couple, is made possible.

---

[18] Gy makes reference to the Gregorian and Gelasian sacramentaries. See Gy, "Le nouveau rituel." The Gelasian only provides the incipit, not the whole text. The whole text used is found in *Le Sacramentaire Grégorien*, ed. Jean Deshusses, Spicilegium Friburgense 16 (Fribourg: n.p., 1971) 309, n. 835. It is also available in *Le formulaire de la messe de mariage du "Sacramentarium Gregorianum" envoyé a Charlemagne par le Pape Hadrien I* (Entre 784/91), in Ritzer, *Le mariage*, 427.

The second formula (no. 235) first appeared in the 1969 order and is now given the thematic title "On the great sacrament of marriage." The text reads in translation:

"It is truly . . . through Christ our Lord: Because in him you have forged a new testament [*testamentum*] with your people, so that humankind whom [the Latin reads simply *quem*] you redeemed by the mysteries of his death and resurrection, you might make partaker of his divine nature and coheir in heaven of his glory. Of the most merciful bounty of this mystery you have made the marriage of man and woman a sign, so that you might recall us to the ineffable plan of your love which this sacrament enacts. And so . . . saying without end."

It is claimed that this fine prayer was inspired by Leo the Great's *Sermo* XXII (On the Nativity), where he discusses the new order of things, the new *dispensatio* inaugurated by the birth of the Son of God.[19] The prayer develops beautifully the covenant theology of marriage. It establishes eloquently the Easter-Church-Marriage relationship.[20] It recalls how God forged a new pact or covenant with God's people, the Church, in the paschal mystery of Christ, through which humanity was made partaker of the divine nature and coheir of heavenly glory. In a phrase evocative of Ephesians 5:21-33, it speaks of the conjugal love of spouses as an image, a *sacramentum* of God's ineffable plan of love. The conjugal covenant reflects God's covenant with his own people.

The third preface (no. 236), like the second, was composed for the 1969 edition and has now been given the thematic title "On marriage, a sign of God's love":

"It is truly . . . to give you thanks: Who willed that humankind whom you created by the gift of your love and mercy [*pietas*] should be raised to such dignity, that you might leave a true image of your love in the union of man and woman: for whom you created from charity, you do not cease to call to the law of charity, so that you might make of humanity a sharer in your eternal charity. While the mystery of this holy marital union is a sign of your love, it makes holy [*sacrat*] human love: through Christ our Lord. Through whom . . . saying without end . . . . ."

[19] Carlo Braga, "La genesi dell'Ordo Matrimonii," *Ephemerides Liturgicae* 93 (1979) 256. See Leo the Great, *Sermo* XXII: PL 54, 193–4.

[20] Franco Brovelli, "La celebrazione del matrimonio," *Rivista Liturgica* 63 (1976) 504.

As the title suggests, the prayer interprets the whole matrimonial experience, indeed the whole of existence, in the light of the vocation of love. Love is humankind's origin, its constant calling, and its fulfillment in heaven. The prayer formula recognizes in the union of husband and wife a genuine and true image of the love of God. The sacrament of marriage, therefore, an abiding sign of God's love, sanctifies or consecrates the love that exists between the husband and wife. In this preface, the phrase "through Christ our Lord" is not put after the opening words of praise but after the expression of the mystery of marriage for which God is thanked. Thus it relates even more forcefully the offering of thanks and the gift of marriage to God's plan in Christ.

These three prefaces bring out the perception of marriage that is incorporated into the Church's great act of thanksgiving. Marriage is consistently referred to as a covenant invested with great dignity. It has been willed by God since creation, a part of God's mysterious divine plan and indeed a special sign of it. God's marvelous action in establishing marriage is precisely one of the things that the preface celebrates or states as reasons for giving thanks. Marriage is a sign, a sacrament of God's unconditional and faithful love for his people. It is for this reason that the conjugal bond is indissoluble. Marriage among the faithful does not only effect the increase of the human community but also brings about the growth of the family of God through baptism. The sacrament is thus placed in its proper ecclesial context. Finally, marriage is, in a unique way, a living out of the universal vocation of love.

TEXTS FOR INTERPOLATIONS IN THE EUCHARISTIC PRAYER

In the 1969 edition of the order, an interpolation for Eucharistic Prayer I, the Roman Canon was provided. The revised edition completes the first by supplying texts for the second and third Eucharistic anaphoras. Nothing is given for Eucharistic Prayer IV because it is not to be used during nuptial masses since the unchangeable preface cannot be replaced by one of the proper prefaces required for marriage. Essentially, these texts are proper intercessions for the bride and groom within the Eucharistic Prayer.

The provision of a formula for the *Hanc igitur* in the Roman Canon is reflective of the tradition in early sacramentaries which gave several variable texts at this point. The text in number 237 of the new order is a conflation of material from the Leonine and Gelasian prayers with the Gregorian.[21] The Latin text may be translated thus:

[21] Stevenson, *To Join Together*, 145.

"Lord, accept this offering from your whole family, and from N. and N. for whom your majesty is entreated: and since you have brought them to their wedding day, (make them rejoice in your gift of desired children), and give to their fruitful years together many descendants. (Through Christ our Lord. Amen)."

The ancient texts focus on the bride, for whom the matron makes the offering. The revised text turns the offering into one made for both woman and man. It no longer refers to specific gifts of the matron but to that of the couple themselves and of the whole community.

The specific request made is that God, who by divine care brought them to the day of their wedding, may continue to watch over them in their marriage. While the earlier texts directed this petition to the procreation of children, the new text refers to their life together into old age. The rubric counsels that when circumstances suggest it the words in parenthesis may be omitted, such as when the couples are no longer capable of having children of their own.

The interpolations for the other two prayers are similar and need not delay us. The interpolation for Eucharistic Prayer II (no. 238) looks to God as the one who has brought the couple to their wedding day. In a simple and direct way it petitions God to "remember" the newlyweds so that with God's grace they may always remain in mutual love and peace. The prayer for the spouses in Eucharistic Prayer III (no. 239) is an appeal for God to strengthen the bride and groom by the grace of matrimony, as well as to keep them faithful, throughout their lives, to the covenant they have sealed in God's sight.

These three formulas attribute to God the authorship of marriage. It is likewise God who appoints the time in which this takes place, who "brings couples to their wedding day." While these texts vary in what they ask for the couple (children, long and happy life, mutual love and peace, fidelity), there is an overwhelming sense of trust in God's power to bring about what is petitioned. Placed in the context of the eucharistic prayer, these interpolations highlight the centrality of the role of the bride and groom in the liturgical celebration. The naming of the couple within this insertion in the anaphora affirms the belief that they truly are the main protagonists, the ministers of the sacrament of matrimony and therefore on this occasion also in the Eucharist, which is offered by the whole community on the occasion of their wedding.

TEXTS FOR THE NUPTIAL BLESSING[22]

There are four formulas for the nuptial blessing in the ROCM, three of which were carried over from the 1969 ritual.[23] Added to these is a new formula for use when the ceremony is presided over by an officially delegated layperson (nos. 139–40). Significant changes to the 1969 texts have been made in the revised edition. Musical annotation has been added, implying that the normative manner of praying them is by chanting.

After the invitation to prayer by the presider, generally the blessing presents a tripartite structure. The first part is the giving of thanks to the creating and redeeming God, in whom marriage and the sacrament originated. The second part evokes old blessings and requests God to repeat his blessings on the new couples, inserting their marriage among the *mirabilia Dei.* To this second part the revised order has added an epiclesis which explicates the request for the outpouring of the Holy Spirit upon the couple. The third section requests God to pour out grace on the bride and bridegroom so that they remain in faith and love and fulfill their matrimonial commitments. Such a structure and content indicate that the nuptial blessing belong to the genre of the Jewish *berakah,* as adapted by the Church.

The first text (nos. 73–4) is a remake of the old formula in the 1570 *Missale Romanum* where it has the following structure: a bidding prayer, a collect, a second invitatory prayer, and the blessing prayer. This consists of three invocations addressed to God the Father, a central petition for the bride, a lengthy series of petitions for certain bridal virtues, a short supplication for the couple, and a conclusion. The text in the 1570 Roman Missal exhibits some similarities with those in ancient Roman sacramentaries. For instance, the introductory collect appears in the *Veronense* (1109) and in the Gregorian (837), placed immediately before the blessing prayer proper. In a slightly modified form it appears as an opening prayer for the nuptial Mass in the Gelasian (1443). The blessing prayer proper in both the *Veronense* (1110) and the *Gelasianum* (1451) is quite different from that of the

---

[22] Studies on the Nuptial Blessing can be found in Enzo Lodi, "La benedizione nuziale. Sua valenza teologico-liturgica," *Rivista Liturgica* 79 (1992) 659–91; Jan Michael Joncas, "Solemnizing the Mystery of Wedded Love: Nuptial Blessings in the *Ordo Celebrandi Matrimonium* 1991," *Worship* 70 (1996) 210–37.

[23] These are found in nos. 73–4, 242, and 243–4.

1570 Missal, except for the petitions on behalf of the bride.[24] The text in the *Missale Romanum*, of course, is a direct recension of the nuptial blessing in the Gregorian (838a-b), and copies it almost verbatim. This 1570 text was then edited for the 1969 edition, which was again touched up during the 1991 revision.

The text of the invitatory reads as follows:

"Let us suppliantly pray to the Lord, dear brethren, that he would mercifully pour out the blessing of his grace upon these servants of his, who are wedded in Christ, and that he would make those he has joined in the holy covenant (and by the sacrament of the Body and Blood of Christ) unified in one love."

The text in the 1570 Missal is of a different genre. It is a prayer addressed to God himself, a collect rather than an invitation to prayer. The 1991 nuptial blessing has slightly modified the 1969 text of the invitatory by making reference to both bride and groom rather than to the bride alone. We now turn to the text of the blessing prayer proper.[25]

"God, who, by the might of your power, have made everything out of nothing; who, in the beginning have set the world in order, and created the human person [*homo* not *vir*] in *your* image, and have ordained woman as the inseparable help of man, so that they should no longer be two, but one flesh, teaching that what you have instituted as one, should never be lawfully put asunder;

"God, who have consecrated conjugal union by so excellent a mystery that you have pre-signified the sacrament of Christ and of the Church in the covenant of marrying people;

"God, through whom woman is joined to man, and through whom their companionship is gifted by a blessing, which alone is not taken away, either by the pain of original sin or by the sentence of the Flood;

"Look kindly upon these servants of yours, who, having been joined in marital partnership, seek to strengthen themselves with your blessing: send forth upon them the grace of the Holy Spirit, so that, with your love diffused in their hearts, they may remain faithful in the conjugal covenant.

[24] See *Veronense* 140 and *Gelasianum* 209–10. Joncas discusses this in "Solemnizing the Mystery," 213–21.

[25] For this translation I have drawn some help from Joncas, "Solemnizing the Mystery," 218–9.

"May the grace of love and peace be *in your female servant N.*, and may she remain an imitator of the holy women whose praises are proclaimed in the Scriptures.

"May the heart of her husband trust in her, who, acknowledging that she is equal in status and co-heir to the life of grace, should offer her honor that is due her and should cherish her always with that love by which Christ cherished his Church.

"And now we pray you, Lord, that these servants of yours might remain, bound in faith, in the commandments and, joined to a single marriage bed, they might be notable for the integrity of their conduct; united by the strength of the Gospel, may they exhibit good testimony to Christ before all (may they be fertile in offspring; may they be parents of tested virtue; may they see their children's children); and, having come at last to a desirable old age, may they come to the life of the blessed and to the heavenly kingdoms. Through Christ our Lord."

The textual modifications on the prayer of the 1570 Roman Missal are quite interesting. First, the reference to the creation of woman from man has been revised to stress the equal status of male and female before God. Second, the names of the Old Testament women have been omitted and are subsumed under a general category. Third, the reference to some of the traditional female virtues has been eliminated and replaced by a section that prays for the bride's activity and life in the Church.

What is retained from the original blessing is the description of marriage as a covenant and sacrament of Christ and his Church. The link between marriage in the order of creation and marriage in the order of redemption is graphically affirmed by the fact that this blessing of conjugal union alone was not wiped away, either through the punishment due original sin or by the sentence of the Flood.

The 1991 text tries to rectify some of the weaknesses or inadequacies that had been noted in the text of 1969. For the first time in the history of the nuptial blessing in the Latin Church, an explicit epiclesis is integrated. There is now in the text a direct invocation that the grace of the Holy Spirit be poured out upon the couple. Musical notes have also been supplied to allow for the chanting of the blessing prayer, which certainly adds more solemnity and dignity to the liturgical action. And, as noted already on the invitatory, there is a shift in the subject of the prayer, which no longer focuses mainly on the bride but on both spouses.

The second nuptial blessing (nos. 241–2), was composed for the 1969 typical edition[26] and made its way into the revised edition with a few alterations. After the invitation to prayer, the formal blessing is composed of two invocations addressed to the Father, a series of petitions for the couple, followed by supplications for the bride and groom individually, and some concluding petitions for both:

"Holy Father, who have created humanity in your image as male and female so that, joined in unity of flesh and heart, man and woman might accomplish their responsibility in the world: God, in order to reveal the plan of your love, made the union of husband and wife an image of the covenant between you and your people, so that in the realization of this sacrament, the marriage of your faithful becomes a sign of the nuptial mystery between Christ and the Church: upon these, your servants (N. and N.) we pray, extend your right hand and *pour out the power of the Holy Spirit into their hearts.* Be present (or grant), Lord, as they begin in the partnership of this sacrament, the gifts of your love may be shared between them, and, manifesting the sign of your presence to one another, they may be one heart and one spirit. Grant also, Lord, that they might sustain by their work the household which they build (they might prepare their children, having been formed by evangelical discipline, to be members of your heavenly family). Deign to bestow on your female servant your blessings, so that, fulfilling the duty of a wife (and mother), she might nourish her household with chaste love and adorn it with affable grace. Deign also to accompany, this, your male servant N. with heavenly blessing so that he might persevere worthily in the responsibilities of a faithful husband (and provident father). Grant, holy Father, that those who have been joined by partnership before you and desire to come to your table may rejoice to share in the heavenly banquet in the future. Through Christ *our Lord. Amen.*"

There are a few modifications introduced by the 1991 text. Most remarkable of these is the insertion of a prayer or epiclesis asking for the outpouring of the power of the Holy Spirit on the couple.

In terms of content, the text underlines the notion of marriage as a covenant between the spouses, a partnership grounded in creation. In a language that harks back to the analogy of the letter to the Ephesians, it sees the union of man and woman in marriage as a symbol of

---

[26] Stevenson names Louis Ligier as the author of a draft of this blessing, which was later edited by Secundo Mazzarello. See *To Join Together,* 130, 145.

the union between God and his people, Christ and his Church. It emphasizes as well the responsibilities of the married couple toward each other, their household, in the Church and in the world. Marriage is looked upon as a locus for growth in holiness in which spouses mutually help each other attain Christian perfection by sharing with each other the gifts of God's love and by being a sign of God's presence to each other. This is heightened by the couple's reception of eucharistic communion hoping that they may in the future rejoice to share in God's eternal banquet. Responsible Christian parenthood is highlighted by the text, underlining the manner in which it should be done; namely, according to the ways of the gospel.

Some critics, however, recognize deficiencies in the text. For instance, there are those who maintain that keeping a "division of labor" or differentiating the separate responsibilities of the spouses may betray a sexist bias.[27] Notwithstanding arguments to the contrary, it seems that "the text as heard in the liturgical assembly suggests that the husband has fewer responsibilities for maintaining the household than does the wife."[28]

Like the second formula, the third was composed for the first typical edition and was adapted in the revised edition. It appears in three versions: one for use by an ordained presider at the marriage between two Christians within or outside the Mass (nos. 243–4), another for use by an ordained presider at marriages between a Catholic and a catechumen or non-Christian (nos. 171–2), and a final one for use by a lay presider (no. 173). When it is used at the marriage between two Christians it begins with an invitation to prayer and then a brief period of silence which is followed by the formal blessing prayer:

"Holy Father, creator of the whole world, who have created man and woman according to your image and have willed that their union be filled to overflowing with your blessing, we humbly pray to you for *these your servants,* who today are joined in the sacrament of marriage. May your abundant blessing, Lord, come down upon *this bride N.,* and upon her partner in life, *N., and may the power of your Holy Spirit from above inflame their hearts* so that, when they are made fruitful by the mutual gift of marriage, they might adorn their family with children and enrich your Church. May they praise you Lord, when they are joyful, seek you when they are sorrowful; may they rejoice that

[27] See Joncas, "Solemnizing Mystery," 223; Stevenson, *To Join Together,* 146.
[28] Joncas, "Solemnizing Mystery," 223.

you are present in their need so that you might sustain them; may they pray to you in the holy assembly; may they exhibit themselves as your witnesses in the world; and having achieved a prosperous old age, with this circle of friends by which they are surrounded, may they come to the heavenly kingdoms. Through Christ *our Lord.*"

In the second edition of this prayer, musical notation is provided for both the invitation to prayer, which is repeated verbatim, and the prayer proper. In the body of the prayer the opening petitions have been reworded so that they apply to the couple throughout the text. There is also a provision for mentioning the name of each spouse. Most significantly, a reference to the Holy Spirit has been inserted, thus transforming it into an epicletic prayer. The formula repeats the themes we have already identified above, such as the establishment of the marriage institution by God as a partnership between a man and a woman; marriage and family serving and enriching the Church; the abiding support and help of God for married people for them to be able to fulfill their responsibilities to one another, to the Church, to society at large, and to God Himself; and marriage as the place in which the spouses grow in holiness.

The second version of this blessing prayer in number 65 is provided for use in a marriage between a Catholic and a non-Christian. In this adapted variant there are a few modifications. At the invitatory the word *sacramento* ("sacrament," "symbol") has been replaced with *consortio* ("partnership"). In the body of the prayer marriage is now referred to as a "covenant" *(foedere)* instead of "sacrament" *(sacramento).* The text about the couple's praying in the holy assembly and witnessing in the world has been omitted. The reference to producing children to enrich the Church has been replaced with a phrase beseeching that they be notable for the integrity of their conduct and be parents of well-tested virtue.

The third version of the third nuptial blessing (no. 173) is provided for use in marriages between a Catholic and a catechumen or non-Christian, presided by a lay assistant. It is a reworking of the previous text and starts off with a benediction of the Creator God, which is a paraphrase of the first paragraph in number 172.[29]

A fourth formula for the nuptial blessing appears for the first time in the 1991 order. It is a text designed for use by a lay presider for

[29] "Blessed are you, Lord God, creator and preserver of the human race, who in the partnership of man and woman, have left a true image of your love."

marriages between two Christians (nos. 139–40). It begins with an invitation to prayer by the lay officiant, and after a short period of silent prayer the prayer proper follows. Quite different from the blessing prayers we have examined so far, the prayer text given here is in a responsorial format, allowing for vocal responses or interventions by the assembly. The intention is to distinguish between a prayer in which a priest or deacon invokes grace upon the couple, and a prayer in which a congregation, led by a lay presider, blesses or praises God for God's works and for benefits received. In a form quite similar to the blessing of baptismal water, there are three exclamations of praise addressed to the persons in the Blessed Trinity, to which the congregation responds, *Benedictus Deus* ("Blessed be God"). The lay presider then concludes with an intercession (two alternatives are given), to which the assembly responds, *Amen.*

The text is as follows, in English translation:

"P: Let us now suppliantly implore the blessing of God upon these spouses, that he might kindly nurture with his help those whom he has joined by the sacrament of marriage.

P: Blessed are you, the Father almighty, who willed to elevate humanity, created by the gift of your piety, to such dignity that in the partnership of man and woman you have left an authentic image of your love.

A: Blessed be God.

P: Blessed are you God, the only-begotten Son, Jesus Christ, who in the conjugal covenant of your faithful willed to reveal the mystery of your love in the Church for whom you handed yourself over that it might be holy and immaculate.

A: Blessed be God.

P: Blessed are you God, the Holy Spirit, Paraclete, worker of all sanctification and maker of unity, who dwell within the children of your delight so that they should take care to preserve unity in the bond of peace.

A: Blessed be God.

P: Grant, Lord, to your servants, N. and N., whom you have joined in the sacrament of matrimony, to be united in mutual love, so that, while they enjoy the gift of marriage, they may adorn the human family with children, enrich the Church, and show themselves your witnesses in the world. Through Christ our Lord.

A: Amen."

Or

"P: Look, Lord, upon these servants of yours, N. and N., and grant, that trusting in you alone, they may receive the gifts of your grace, preserve charity in unity, and may merit to come, after the course of this life, to the joys of eternal happiness, one with their children. Through Christ our Lord.
A: Amen."

It is praiseworthy that an alternative way of pronouncing the nuptial blessing that can be used by a lay presider has been made available. This form unquestionably enhances the full, conscious, and active participation of the liturgical assembly. It is lamentable, however, that this prayer text has not been provided with musical notation.

Symbols or Gestures Accompanying the Nuptial Blessing

The accompanying rubrics specify that while the nuptial blessing is given, that is, chanted or recited, the spouses kneel before the altar (during Mass) or at their place (outside Mass). From the old liturgical tradition kneeling has always been looked upon as an imprecatory posture. It is literally a posture of begging, of making oneself low to emphasize the attitude of humility that accompanies the request. It is thus a gesture of readiness to receive blessings from God.

While giving the blessing, ordained presiders extend their hands over the spouses. Lay presiders keep their hands joined as they chant or recite the ascriptions of praise and collect. The extension of hands, without a doubt, highlights the epicletic character of the prayer. One can easily call to mind some parallels, such as the use of the gesture at the recitation of the Last Supper narrative in the Eucharist or in conjunction with the solemn prayer of blessing during priestly and episcopal ordinations. It signifies quite palpably the coming down of the Holy Spirit and the Spirit's gifts. Some, however, have voiced their dissatisfaction over the attempt to clearly distinguish the ordained from the lay presider in the instruction that the latter is to pronounce the nuptial blessing over the spouses with joined hands.[30]

In speaking of the modifications introduced in 1991 on the formulas of the nuptial blessing, two things seem to emerge. One is the decision to make the blessing address both spouses throughout, already hinted at by the change of the title of the prayer. In the OCM the prayer is called *Oratio Super Sponsam et Sponsum.* The ROCM simply

[30] Joncas questions the wisdom of this rubric in his article "Solemnizing the Mystery," 232.

refs to it as *Benedictio Nuptialis*. The other and more significant change is the addition of an epiclesis, not only to underline the indispensable role of the Holy Spirit but also to transform this formula into a genuine epicletic prayer.[31] This is intensified by the kneeling posture of the spouses and the extension of hands by the ordained presider over them. These emendations express the desire to rectify the inadequacies of the first typical edition.

Basically, the blessing formulas present the same marriage themes. There is a recognition of the establishment of the marriage institution by God as a partnership between a man and a woman. This partnership has its foundations already in creation, which was never abrogated, neither by original sin nor by the Flood. They highlight the sacramental nature of Christian marriage. They speak of the mission of the spouses and the family they are going to build toward the Church and the human community at large. With the grace and power of the Holy Spirit, married people are assured of the abiding support and help of God for them to be able to fulfill their responsibilities. Marriage and the family then are places in which the spouses can grow in holiness.

BLESSINGS AT THE END OF MASS

For the blessing at the conclusion of the nuptial Mass three texts are offered, all of which come from the text of 1969. These prayers have been influenced by the 1950 German rite of marriage, which drew inspiration from the Visigothic liturgy, particularly in this part.[32] All three formulas are made up of a series of three blessing sentences for the spouses, to each of which the assembly responds "Amen." The fourth sentence is a stereotyped concluding blessing for the whole liturgical assembly.

---

[31] While the introduction of an epiclesis into the nuptial blessing has been lauded by many commentators, Adrian Nocent gives a dissenting opinion. He argues that this might create confusion, that is, giving the impression that this is the most essential part, and hence will not result in the enrichment of the theology of marriage. Inserting an epiclesis into the nuptial blessing gives it great importance and tends to sacramentalize it as, in fact, has happened in history. He goes on to suggest the omission of such epiclesis in the nuptial blessing and that some sort of epicletic prayer be pronounced over the couple before the exchange of consent. See his review of the ROCM in "La nouvelle édition du rituel du mariage," *Ecclesia Orans* 8 (1991) 330–4.

[32] Brovelli, "La celebrazione del matrimonio," 505.

The first option (no. 248) is based on a longer version which can be found in the Spanish *Liber Ordinum*.[33] The Visigothic efflorescence, however, has been toned down. The texts are theocentric and pastoral. They wish for mutual love, peace in the home, the blessing of children, and comfort of friends, witnessing to God's love in the world through service to the poor and suffering, in view of entering the eternal home of God.

The second option (no. 249) was composed for the 1969 typical edition. Although it is Visigoth-based structurally, it now follows a Trinitarian pattern, that is, each of the three blessing sentences invokes one of the three persons in the Holy Trinity. The structure and pattern seem quite creative, but the contents of the blessings appear to be a little problematic. The different tasks assigned to each of the Trinitarian persons do not seem to be entirely consistent with the doctrine of the economic trinity. For example, the Father is asked to bestow on the couples joy and blessing in the gift of children, the Son for assistance and mercy at all times, and the Holy Spirit for love to fill their hearts.

The last formula (no. 250), together with the second, first appeared in the 1969 edition. The blessing sentences invoke the name of the Lord Jesus. It begins by evoking the presence of the Lord at the marriage in Cana. As the Lord blessed that wedding with his presence, so it is asked that he would also bless the newlyweds, their families, and their friends. Invoking Christ's eternal love for the Church, appeal is also made that Christ's love be poured into the spouses' hearts. With an eschatological note, the third blessing sentence mentions the couple's belief in the resurrection as a motive for asking that they may await the Lord's return with joyful hope.

These formulas for the solemn blessing repeat many of the marriage themes already found in the texts of the nuptial blessing. Although there is no rubric prescribing that the priest or deacon extends his hands over the spouses, it can be presumed that he must do so

[33] The *Liber Ordinum* is a collection of Spanish or Visigothic rites which was specially put together for presentation to Pope Alexander II in 1056 in order to prevent the Romanization of the (now reconquered) regions of Spain which had preserved for centuries their own native liturgical customs and traditions under centuries of Arab rule and were now threatened with losing them. Texts can be found in M. Férotin, ed., *Le Liber Ordinum en usage dans l'église wisigothique et mozarabe d'Espagne du cinquième au onzième siècle*, Mon. eccles. lit. 5 (Paris: Firmin-Didot, 1904) 433–43. English translation is supplied in Mark Searle and Kenneth Stevenson, *Documents of the Marriage Liturgy* (Collegeville: The Liturgical Press, 1992) 122–34.

insofar as these blessings belong to the genre of the solemn blessings in the Sacramentary. In this case, would these blessings not appear to be simply duplicating the nuptial blessing?

CONCLUSION

The Scripture readings and euchological texts for the liturgical celebration of marriage highlight some theological themes which lead to a better understanding of the Church's teaching on the meaning of Christian marriage.

Consistent with the liturgical principle maintaining that the Word is a principal element of every liturgical celebration, the revised order of 1991 provides a substantial number of lectionary texts. Although only a few of these explicitly speak about marriage, the whole selection is helpful in accentuating certain aspects of the sacrament.

What is highlighted, first of all, is the sacramentality of the marriage covenant, often referred to as a symbol of the covenantal relationship between God and God's people, and between Christ and the Church. This conjugal covenant entered into by a man and a woman reaches its highpoint in eucharistic communion, which seals it. It is for this reason that the order stresses that the normative way of celebrating marriage among the baptized is *intra Missam*. The Eucharist, which celebrates the paschal mystery of Christ, is both a sacramental model and an efficacious symbol of the marital union.

Because marriage has its origin in God, who willed and blessed the union of man and woman in creation, marriage, whose blessing was never abrogated either by original sin or the Flood, has a place in God's mysterious plan of salvation. As Christ has raised it to the category of a sacrament, marriage enjoys God's continued blessing.

The Scripture and euchological texts suitably locate matrimony in an ecclesial framework. In bringing forth children, couples do not only adorn the world. Through the sacrament of baptism, they also cause the growth of the family of God, the Church. At the same time marriage, in its unique and particular way, is a concrete realization of the universal Christian vocation of love; love being humanity's origin and end. Married couples are called upon to give witness to this love in their relationship with one another in the family, in the Church, and in the world. In this manner the missionary dimension of marriage is fulfilled. For its part, however, the Church community has the responsibility of assisting couples so that they remain true to their vocation as Christian spouses and parents.

Although the texts themselves do not use these terms, one might say that they speak of Christian couples as having the duty to establish their families as genuine "domestic Churches," that is, as "schools of holiness" both for the spouses themselves and for their children. As "co-creators" with God, spouses commit themselves to procreation and the formation of their children, within the family, according to Gospel values.

The revision of 1991 tries to address some of the theological and liturgical deficiencies by filling in some of the lacunae and by introducing some novelties. Most significant is the introduction or insertion of an explicit epiclesis into the texts of the nuptial blessing. This manifests a recognition of the indispensable role of the Holy Spirit in the celebration as well as the living out of this sacrament. In addition, consonant with its nature as a solemn epicletic prayer, the revised order has suitably provided musical notes, indicating the preferred manner in which it is to be prayed. It has been found appropriate to modify some of the texts in order to emphasize the mutual responsibility of husbands and wives.

The texts make clear that the spouses are the main protagonists of the celebration, the ministers of the sacrament. Equally emphasized, however, is the essential role of the liturgical assembly led by its officially designated witnesses, representing the whole community of the Church. The revisions and novelties make possible the full and active participation of the whole liturgical assembly. Flexibility is another characteristic of the revised typical edition, as evidenced by the ample selections provided allowing for great liturgical creativity as well as adaptation in various circumstances. In fact, it is made clear that in most cases the texts are provided simply as models; hence, room is given for the creation of new ones adapted to particular situations or instances.

Chapter IV

Inculturation and Contextualization

In the preceding chapters we examined the revised typical edition of the *Ordo Celebrandi Matrimonium* of the Roman Rite. In the present chapter we will consider the principles involved in developing a liturgy suited to a particular culture that is built on the traditions of the Roman liturgy as well as on this culture.

In the first part of the chapter we note the principles in the 1994 instruction of the Congregation for Divine Worship and the Discipline of Sacraments, *The Roman Liturgy and Inculturation,*[1] that are appropriate to the inculturation of marriage rites. To complement the processes described in the document, this is followed by a look at the methods of inculturation proffered by Anscar Chupungco; namely, dynamic equivalence, creative assimilation, and organic progression. Third and finally, note is taken of the complementary method of contextualization as it is developed by some Filipino writers. While that has the Church in the Philippines particularly in mind, the method is of interest to all countries where the work of inculturation must embody a retrieval of ancient customs and traditions, while being sensitive to current changes in cultural climate.

---

[1] This document was published simultaneously in several European languages. For the English text see Congregation for Divine Worship and the Discipline of the Sacraments, *The Roman Liturgy and Inculturation,* 4th Instruction for the Right Application of the Constitution on the Liturgy (nos. 37–40) (Rome: Vatican Press, 1994). Henceforth this will be quoted as *Instruction on Inculturation.* For the Latin text see Congregatio de Cultu Divino et Disciplina Sacramentorum, "De Liturgia Romana et Inculturatione. Instructio Quarta 'Ad Exsecutionem Constitutionis Concilii Vaticani Secundi de Sacra Liturgia Recte Ordinandam' (Ad Const. Art. 37–40)," *Notitiae* XXX (1994) 80–115. Henceforth this will be quoted as *Varietates legitimae.*

LITURGICAL INCULTURATION

The Roman Instruction on Liturgical Inculturation[2]

On January 25, 1994, the Sacred Congregation for Divine Worship and the Discipline of the Sacraments published an instruction, the fourth of its kind, for the right application of the Constitution on the Liturgy of Vatican II. This deals with articles 37 through 40 of the Constitution, which have to do with liturgy's relation to cultures. Envisaged to give clearer and more precise definitions and explanations of the principles involved in the task of inserting the liturgy into the various cultures and traditions of peoples,[3] this document likewise sets out authoritatively and definitively the rules, order, and methodology to be followed "so that in the future this will be considered the only correct procedure."[4]

The genesis of the document, as described by Pedro Rocha,[5] shows that it was prepared over a period of time, with some consultation of bishops and liturgical commissions around the world. On the one hand, it is intended to carry forward the ideas expressed by Pope John Paul II on the inculturation of the Gospel and of the liturgy. On the other, it is meant to address the situation that has emerged due to revisions and experiments in liturgical inculturation that have been

---

[2] In printing the instruction, *Notitiae* accompanied it with a presentation of the document by the Secretary of the Congregation, Geraldo M. Agnelo, and with an unsigned commentary. See Geraldo M. Agnelo, "Liturgia Romana e inculturazione," *Notitiae* XXX (1994) 71–7, and "'Commentarium' alla quarta istruzione per una corretta applicazione della costituzione conciliare sulla sacra liturgia," *Notitiae* XXX (1994) 152–66. Other commentaries may be found in Anscar Chupungco, "Remarks on 'The Roman Liturgy and Liturgical Inculturation,'" *Ecclesia Orans* 11 (1994) 269–77; Pierre Jounel, "Une étape majeure sur le chemin de l'inculturation liturgique," *Notitiae* XXX (1994) 260–77. Chupungco's role in preparing the instruction makes his commentary particularly useful.

[3] In no. 2, the instruction quotes the task proposed by John Paul II in the Apostolic Letter of 1989, *Vicesimus quintus annus:* "Summus Pontifex Ioannes Paulus II conatum inserendi in variis culturis tamquam officium magni ponderis ad liturgicam instaurationem exsequendam considerat." See *AAS* 81 (1989) 912. The English text translates *inserendi* as "take root," rather than "insert."

[4] *Varietates legitimae* 3.

[5] The document's genesis is presented by Pedro Rocha, "Liturgia e inculturazione (Dalla Const. *Sacrosanctum Concilium* [SC] all'istruzione *Varietates legitimae* [VL])," *Studia Missionalia* 44 (1995) 149–68. See also Kenneth J. Martin, "Genetic and Analytic Study of the 'Roman Liturgy and Inculturation: Fourth Instruction for the Right Application of the Conciliar Constitution on the Liturgy (nn. 37–40)'" (S.T.L. thesis, Catholic University of America, Washington, D.C., 1996).

carried out in places such as Thailand, Zaire (now the Democratic Republic of the Congo), and Japan. It is the belief of the Roman Congregation that the developing situation requires more carefully enunciated theological principles and practical directives.

The instruction consists of four parts. In the first part, after a brief introduction on the nature of the document and preliminary observations on inculturation in general, it traces the process of inculturation throughout salvation history. The second part is devoted to a description of the theological requirements emerging from the nature of liturgy and the preliminary conditions for liturgical inculturation. In the third section the principles and practical norms for the inculturation of the Roman Rite are outlined. As commentators have noted, this indicates that it is not the instruction's intention to treat the practical aspects of all liturgical inculturation, but only those relating to the Roman Rite, to which it gives a privileged place throughout the Western world and in countries evangelized by missionaries from the Western world.[6] In this part of the instruction the language changes back from that of inculturation to that of adaptation *(aptatio)*. The fourth and final section identifies the areas in the Roman Rite which are open to inculturation as well as the procedure to be followed in making adaptations provided for in the liturgical books or as proposed by the conferences of bishops. It also makes mention of the more radical changes that may be exacted by the genius and traditions of particular peoples, envisaged in SC 40, but it does not give a detailed description of what this would involve in changing texts and rites.

The Gospel and Culture in Dialogue

The document reiterates the Church's commitment to respecting the various cultures of peoples in its mission of evangelization, particularly as enunciated in the documents of Vatican II. Quoting the Pope's encyclical letter *Slavorum Apostoli*,[7] it makes reference to his use of the term "inculturation" to designate the process by which the Gospel is incarnated in autonomous cultures while peoples and their cultures are at the same time introduced into the life of the Church.[8] It is preferred to "adaptation," an expression borrowed from missionary

---

[6] See Chupungco, "Remarks," 272–3, and Jounel, "Une étape majeure," 274–5.

[7] John Paul II, Encyclical Letter *Slavorum Apostoli*, 2 June 1985, no. 21: *AAS* 77 (1985) 802–3.

[8] *Varietates legitimae* 4.

terminology, because the latter connotes "modifications of a somewhat transitory and external nature."[9] Inculturation, on the contrary,
implies a more dynamic, creative, and profound process. It signifies
"an intimate transformation of the authentic cultural values by their
integration into Christianity and the implantation of Christianity into
different human cultures."[10] It designates a double movement, a mutual interaction, a reciprocal assimilation between the Gospel and the
various cultures. This twofold action has already been noted in the
statement made as a result of the 1985 Extraordinary Synod of Bishops
when it was declared:

"Since the Church is a communion which joins diversity and unity,
being present throughout the world, it takes up whatever it finds
positive in all cultures. Inculturation, however, is different from a
mere external adaptation as it signifies an interior transformation of
authentic cultural values through integration into Christianity and the
rooting of Christianity in various human cultures."[11]

The instruction underscores that in reading articles 37 through 40 of
the Constitution on the Liturgy, as well as the rest of the paragraphs
which speak of "liturgical adaptation," they have to be understood in
this sense. The Second Vatican Council did not promote a superficial
interaction between the Gospel and culture in order to modify the external shape and form of the liturgy. What it called for was a reciprocal
assimilation which results in mutual enrichment, that is, transformation of culture and the cultural rooting of the Christian faith.

It advocated a mutually respectful interaction, recognizing that
both have something positive to contribute toward the growth and
well-being of the people of God. Although a wholesale appropriation
of culture and its elements is not advanced, what is significant is the
appreciative awareness of the wisdom and genius found in the cultural traditions of various peoples.

[9] Ibid.

[10] John Paul II, Encyclical Letter *Redemptoris Missio*, 7 December 1990, no. 52:
AAS 83 (1991) 300. Quoted in *Varietates legitimae* 4. The Latin reads *radicatio,* which
means "taking root" rather than "implantation." The text of the encyclical has
been slightly altered by the instruction so as to read *radicatio christianismi* rather
than *nominis christiani insertio.*

[11] Synod of Bishops, Final Report *Exeunte coetu secundo,* 7 December 1985, D. 4;
cited in Anscar Chupungco, *Liturgical Inculturation* (Collegeville: The Liturgical
Press, 1992) 29.

Liturgical inculturation is one aspect of the task of rooting the Gospel in people's cultures. It is a facet of the overall attempt to integrate the Christian message into their faith life and the permanent values of their culture.[12] Because the liturgy cannot afford to be an extraneous element in the Christian life of any nation or people, it should be capable of expressing itself in every human culture while maintaining its identity and transcending the particularity of race and nation.[13] Even as it opens itself to adaptation, the liturgy must remain faithful to the Christian tradition. In the process of inculturation not only are human cultures and traditions given respect and appreciation by the Church's liturgy. They are also purified and sanctified, strengthened and ennobled, raised up and made perfect.[14]

Due to the complexity and importance of the task, the document reminds the reader that this should not be undertaken haphazardly but with the aid of methodical research and ongoing discernment.[15] This is necessary "so that through the liturgy the work of salvation accomplished by Christ may continue faithfully in the Church by the power of the Spirit, in different countries and times and in different human cultures."[16] This it takes to have been exemplified by the process of inculturation in the early Church, which it briefly surveys.[17]

Theological Principles Arising from the Nature of the Liturgy

Liturgical inculturation, the document points out, is not an end in itself. It is grounded in theological principles which issue from the nature and purpose of the liturgy itself. Differently put, inculturation is a theological and a liturgical imperative. The instruction mentions several principles which are to be borne in mind while accomplishing this work.

In the first place, the liturgy is "at once the action of Christ the priest and the action of the Church which is his body,"[18] it is the worship of the whole Church, the *totus Christus*, head and members.

---

[12] *Varietates legitimae* 5.
[13] *Varietates legitimae* 18.
[14] LG 13 and 17; also quoted in *Varietates legitimae* 18.
[15] LG 5.
[16] LG 20.
[17] LG 9–20.
[18] LG 21.

Second, the document cites the ecclesial character of the liturgy. In essence it is a disclosure of the Church and its nature as a "catholic" or universal community of pilgrims called by God in the Holy Spirit, waiting in joyful hope for the Lord's Second Coming (Titus 2:13).[19] On the one hand, an inculturated liturgy should never be one that showcases the rites and traditions of a particular culture at the expense of the faith of the Church. On the other hand, if the Church itself is mediated in the liturgy the celebrating community must be able to relate and identify with its language and symbols.

Third, in the liturgy the Church is nourished on the Word of God because it is God who speaks when the Sacred Scriptures are proclaimed.[20] This undergirds the pride of place which they enjoy in the Church and their importance in liturgical celebration.

The fourth principle echoes paragraph 7 of the Constitution on the Liturgy, which declares that the liturgy is always the celebration of the paschal mystery of Christ, whereby God is glorified and humanity is sanctified.[21] Inculturation should never gloss over this fundamental principle but must enhance it.

Fifth, the liturgical life of the Church gravitates chiefly around the eucharistic sacrifice and the other sacraments. In dispensing this task, of which inculturation is part, it has to recognize that there are unchangeable parts of the liturgy; namely, those which are directly related to the will of Christ. These constitute the elements of the liturgy determined by Christ, over which the Church has no power.[22]

Rephrasing numbers 28 and 26 of *Lumen Gentium*, the sixth principle states that the Church of Christ is signified and made present by the liturgical assembly in a given place and a given time.[23] In other words, through the liturgy the local church reveals the Church in its true nature. This expresses the particular church's unity with the universal Church not only in faith and sacraments,[24] but also in practices

[19] LG 22.

[20] *Varietates legitimae* 23. The document quotes SC 7.

[21] *Varietates legitimae* 24.

[22] *Varietates legitimae* 25. The document here refers to SC 21.

[23] *Varietates legitimae* 26.

[24] Chupungco, "Remarks," 272, claims that the English version of this paragraph is defective because it has "in belief and sacramentals" where it should read "in faith and sacraments." Even Chupungco's translation is not exact. The Latin reads *quoad fidei doctrinam et signa sacramentalia,* which is more exactly rendered, "in the doctrine of the faith and in sacramental signs."

handed down by apostolic tradition, such as Sunday observance, celebration of Easter, daily prayer, penance, and the other sacraments. While preserving and safeguarding the unity between the local and the universal Church, there is the need for the liturgy to become native to every culture. As one might say, certain accommodations have to be made to bear the mark of each culture in order for the liturgy to become a part of the people's "webs of significance," to use the phrase of cultural anthropologist Clifford Geertz.

The seventh and final principle affirms that the liturgy expresses the faith of the Church in a symbolic and communitarian form, and needs the supervision by the appropriate authority of the organization of worship, the preparation of texts, and the celebration of rites.[25]

Principles Emerging from Culture

Because inculturation is a dialogical encounter between the liturgy and a given local culture, the instruction addresses the principles and conditions arising from the side of culture.

First of all, it emphasizes the indispensability of using the people's own language in the work of evangelization, as the Church's missionary tradition has shown. This is a fundamental principle in inculturation since "it is by the mother language, which conveys the mentality and the culture of a people, that one can reach the soul, mould it in the Christian spirit, and allow it to share more deeply in the prayer of the Church."[26]

Second, it notes that the degree and form of inculturation to be applied is dependent on the situations of local churches.[27] The instruction mentions in general some of these situations and the approaches which might be taken. In the first place, it has in mind the young churches or countries which do not have a Christian tradition and where the Gospel was proclaimed by missionaries who brought with them the Roman Rite. The operating principle is for the Church "to welcome all that can be reconciled with the gospel in the tradition of a

---

[25] *Varietates legitimae* 27. The Instruction refers to the Roman Missal, General Introduction, Prooemium, no. 2, which says of itself: "In this new Missal then, the church's rule of prayer *(lex orandi)* corresponds to its constant rule of faith *(lex credendi)*." It also quotes Paul VI's Discourse to the Consilium for the Application of the Constitution on the Liturgy, October 13, 1966: *AAS* 58 (1966) 1146; October 14, 1968: *AAS* 60 (1968) 734.

[26] *Varietates legitimae* 28. This echoes no. 53 of Pope John Paul II's Encyclical Letter *Redemptoris Missio* 7 December 1990: *AAS* 83 (1991) 300–2.

[27] *Varietates legitimae* 29.

people, to bring it to the riches of Christ, and to be enriched in turn by the many different forms of wisdom of the nations on earth."[28] For countries which were evangelized centuries ago and where the Christian faith continues to influence the culture, "the possibilities of adaptation envisaged in the liturgical books *should* [*sic*], on the whole, be considered sufficient to allow for legitimate local diversity."[29] For countries where several cultures coexist, especially as a result of immigration, the instruction recommends a more prudent approach, that is, to take account first of all of the particular problems this situation poses.[30] Each culture and people, including minorities, are to be respected and studied with care. However, we should be wary of the tendency to be inward looking or of the temptation to use inculturation for political ends.[31] As for those communities where culture is marked by indifference or disinterest in religion, the document recommends that this be addressed not so much through inculturation as through liturgical formation.[32] There are those who think, however, that this should neither be read in a mutually exclusive fashion nor understood in a temporal sequence, that is, formation before inculturation.[33] Liturgical inculturation and formation must go hand in hand. Not only does an inculturated liturgy enhance liturgical formation, it is in itself a useful means of evangelization.

Third, the instruction calls attention to the reality of cultural change. Culture is a dynamic not a static reality. It is in the process of constant evolution, especially when "affected by an urban and industrial culture" of more recent innovation.[34]

---

[28] *Varietates legitimae* 6. The quotation was taken from Pope John Paul II's "Discourse to the Plenary Assembly of the Pontifical Council for Culture," 17 January 1987, no. 5: *AAS* 79 (1987) 1204.

[29] *Varietates legitimae* 7. Chupungco is of the opinion that the English version mistranslated this sentence, "the measures of adaptation envisaged in the liturgical books were considered [*sic*], on the whole sufficient . . . ." The Latin text reads *pares esse videntur,* that is, the adaptations foreseen in the liturgical books seem on a whole to be sufficient to the task of inculturation. He also notes that for churches of western tradition the Instruction does not close the door to that type of inculturation which is not envisaged by the liturgical books. See Chupungco, "Remarks," 273.

[30] *Varietates legitimae* 7.

[31] *Varietates legitimae* 49.

[32] *Varietates legitimae* 8.

[33] See Chupungco, "Remarks," 273.

[34] *Varietates legitimae* 30.

Fourth, the document makes clear that inculturation is a concerted effort. Episcopal conferences are advised to seek the collaboration of competent scholars in the field of liturgy as well as in the field of local cultural customs and values.[35] The necessary preliminary historical, anthropological, exegetical, and theological studies should be carried out in the light of the pastoral experience of the local clergy, especially the native born who certainly have a sense of their own culture. It also adds that the advice of "wise people" of the country, whose wisdom is enriched by the light of the Gospel, can be helpful. Inculturation, however, is not an exercise in anachronism. That is why the instruction directs the competent local authorities not to allow into the liturgy elements which contribute to confusion rather than to deeper understanding and appreciation by the faithful.

General Principles and Practical Norms

THREE GENERAL PRINCIPLES

The third section of the document (nos. 33–51) turns to the Roman Rite and identifies the general principles and specifies the practical norms or guidelines for its inculturation. The general principles which are mentioned are not new. For the most part, the instruction is simply recapitulating what the Constitution on the Liturgy of Vatican II laid down earlier, but does so with greater force. Without going into the details of this section of the document, it is helpful to note some practical principles that pertain to marriage rites.

Paragraphs 38 through 45 set forth the areas or celebration in which adaptations are suitably made. Foremost, the document mentions *language,* reminding us that the use of the people's own language is a key element since language is a major determinant of culture. While this will mean not only finding the right words but also embracing poetic and rhetorical styles of diverse peoples, on the side of tradition the instruction reminds us to take account of the various literary genres used in the liturgy, such as biblical texts, presidential prayers, psalmody, acclamations, refrains, responsories, hymns, and litanies.[36]

Because of the pride of place they enjoy, music and singing are to be promoted. Reiterating *Sacrosanctum Concilium* 119, the instruction speaks of the need to appreciate the musical traditions of peoples,

[35] *Varietates legitimae* 30.
[36] *Varietates legitimae* 39.

especially in the missions where these play a great part in their religious and social lives. Taking a cue from *Sacrosanctum Concilium* 120, it allows for the usage of local musical forms and melodies, and local musical instruments as well, provided they are appropriate and are in accord with the dignity of the worship space, contributing to the edification and inspiration of the faithful.[37]

On the subject of *gestures* and *postures*, what is pointed out is the need to preserve, as they have been determined by the Holy See, those which belong to the essential rites of the sacraments, and which are required for validity.[38] Gestures and postures native to the local churches may be admitted to the liturgy, provided they have a sense of the sacred, that is, they "express the attitude of humanity before God" and are somehow related with those in the Bible.[39] They should be expressions of genuine prayer and not simply performances. Some of the forms of external expression which might be adopted in the liturgy include hand clapping, rhythmic swaying, and dance movements.[40]

Art is another area in which the riches and genius of the various cultures can be brought to bear in the liturgy. The document cannot be more encouraging in this regard than when it says, "Preference should be given to materials, forms and colors which are in use in the country."[41] Care must be taken that the arts enhance the beauty of the liturgy and that pieces of art used are genuinely significant in the life and tradition of the people.[42]

The instruction, following the principles enunciated in *Sacrosanctum Concilium* 13, warns against the introduction of devotional practices into liturgical celebrations under the guise of inculturation.[43] Although their value in the faith-life of the faithful is acknowledged especially when they are purified and permeated with the Gospel, the local ordinary is to see that these devotions neither replace nor get mixed up with the liturgical celebrations insofar as by its nature the liturgy is superior to them.[44]

[37] *Varietates legitimae* 39.

[38] *Varietates legitimae* 41. See also CIC, can. 841.

[39] *Varietates legitimae* 41.

[40] *Varietates legitimae* 42.

[41] *Varietates legitimae* 43. The document makes reference to SC 123–4 and CIC, can. 1216.

[42] *Varietates legitimae* 43.

[43] *Varietates legitimae* 45.

[44] *Varietates legitimae* 45. This prescription has been expressed earlier in Pope John Paul II's Apostolic Letter *Vicesimus quintus annus,* 4 December 1988, no. 18:

Areas of Inculturation in the Roman Rite

In the fourth section the instruction identifies the areas in the Roman Rite in which the process of inculturation may occur. In the first part (nos. 53–61), the adaptations provided for in the liturgical books are discussed, while the second part (nos. 63–4) treats the more profound adaptations not envisaged by the liturgical books which are possible in certain circumstances especially in mission countries. Each type of inculturation is followed by a well-defined procedure detailing how to go about the process. Covered in this first type are the sacraments (particularly the Eucharist, baptism, confirmation, and marriage) and sacramentals (such as funerals, blessings, the liturgical year, and the Liturgy of the Hours).

On marriage in particular the instruction notes that in a good number of places it is this rite "that calls for the greatest degree of adaptation so as not to be foreign to social customs."[45] In this regard, episcopal conferences are to draw up their own marriage rites satisfying the demands of the law that the ordained minister or the assisting layperson asks for, obtain the consent of the contracting parties, and give them the nuptial blessing.[46] Aside from these requirements, it is also desired that the proper rite responds to the criteria specified in *Sacrosanctum Concilium* 77; namely, that it brings out clearly the Christian meaning of marriage, emphasizes the grace of the sacrament, and underlines the duties of the spouses.[47]

INCULTURATION NOT ENVISAGED
IN THE PUBLISHED LITURGICAL BOOKS

Paragraphs 63 through 69 discuss inculturation of the more radical type, allowing for changes not provided for in the liturgical books.

AAS 81 (1989) 914. On popular devotions, Chupungco makes this insightful remark: "One thing is incorporating popular devotions wholesale into the liturgy, and another is employing their language and ritual patterns for the sake of a more popular and less classical form of worship. This may prove valuable in places where popular devotions are a vibrant element of religious life." See Chupungco, "Remarks," 276.

[45] *Varietates legitimae* 57.

[46] This is a ruling enunciated in the Code of Canon Law (canons 1108 and 112), SC 77, and in the ROCM's *praenotanda* (no. 42).

[47] We have already seen the provisions made for the use of people's own rites in the *Ordo Celebrandi Matrimonium*, as well as the importance given to retention of the nuptial blessing.

This concerns cases already envisaged by *Sacrosanctum Concilium* 40, which states that "in some places and circumstances, an even more radical adaptation of the liturgy is needed and this entails greater difficulties." Before resorting to this type of inculturation, however, all the possibilities offered by the liturgical books have to be exhausted. A study, evaluation, and, if need be, revision of the adaptations that have been introduced is to be made by episcopal conferences before proceeding to more drastic modifications.[48] But how radical could they go? The instruction does not really provide much room because of the boundaries it sets. It makes clear that "adaptations of this kind do not envisage a transformation of the Roman rite, but are made within the context of the Roman rite."[49] This implies that even after a liturgical rite has undergone the process of inculturation beyond those offered in the typical edition, it should still be recognized as a rite of the Latin Church, its Roman character still intact. In undertaking this task the conferences of bishops are to work under the guidance of the Congregation for Divine Worship and the Discipline of the Sacraments who will assist them "in a spirit of confident collaboration and shared responsibility."[50]

The procedure to be followed described in paragraphs 65 through 69 is a reworking of the process already described in *Sacrosanctum Concilium* 40, but this time it is more specific and more descriptive. The episcopal conferences through the national or regional commissions study and examine, with suitable advice from experts, what has to be modified in the liturgical celebrations in view of the people's traditions and worldview. The same is to be done with the local culture, analyzing and determining which elements may be admitted to the liturgy.[51] A proposal—which includes description of innovations proposed, reasons for their adoption, criteria used, the times, places, and people involved for the initial experimentation, the acts of the discussion, and the vote of the conference—is then presented to the congregation. After an examination of the proposal and if found appropriate, the congregation grants the episcopal conference a faculty to make an experiment for a definite period.[52] When the period of experimentation is over, the episcopal conference makes an evaluation

[48] *Varietates legitimae* 63.
[49] *Varietates legitimae* 63.
[50] *Varietates legitimae* 64.
[51] *Varietates legitimae* 65.
[52] *Varietates legitimae* 66.

of the process in view of the goals proposed or necessary revisions. The conclusions, together with the full information about the experiment, are submitted to the congregation which, after examining the report, can give its consent through a decree allowing certain changes to be introduced into the liturgical rite for the region covered by the conference.[53] Meanwhile, all the faithful are to be fully informed about the changes and prepared for their introduction into the inculturated liturgical celebrations.

THE INSTRUCTION: AN INCOMPLETE DOCUMENT

The document is undeniably a step forward, a development in liturgical renewal. It certainly is a help for conferences of bishops and liturgical commissions in their effort to make the liturgy more relevant and more meaningful to the faithful. It has supplied authoritative guidance and clarifications concerning the nature, purpose, governing principles, and process of inculturation. The document in itself is a manifestation of the Church's respectful, benevolent, and welcoming attitude toward culture. It is not difficult to see the attempt to maintain a balanced approach to culture, cultural diversity, and cultural evolution. The document, however, is far from complete. The big lacuna is that it does not address the question of methodology in spite of the fact that it provides the important principles and detailed directions on how to proceed with the task. Besides, the instruction seems to have a very narrow or restrictive understanding of inculturation when it turns to the use of the Roman Rite, when even the vocabulary turns back to that of adaptation. It does treat of creativity, of the creation of new rites and texts. However, when note is taken of the other parts of the document, it follows that this is not excluded in principle.[54]

[53] *Varietates legitimae* 67–8.

[54] Pierre Jounel also notes that in its second part, *Varietates legitimae* treats only of adaptations to the Roman Rite and gives incomplete treatment to the deeper revisions foreseen by SC 40. See Jounel, "Une étape majeure," 276–7. Agnelo notes that the treatment on this point is brief, but sees this as a legislative prudence, since the inculturation envisioned in SC 40 is a field not yet greatly explored. See "Liturgia romana e inculturazione," 76–7. This opinion is shared by the following authors: Joan M. Canals, "Realizaciones de inculturación en la liturgia romana," *Phase* XXXV (1995) 113–26, esp. 123–6; José L. Yáñez, "La inculturación en la liturgia: Comentario desde América," *Phase* XXXV (1995) 135–42. The unsigned commentary in *Notitiae* notes that the revision foreseen in the instruction is to take place within the Roman Rite, but affirms the adequacy of these parameters for all work of liturgical inculturation. See "'Commentarium' alla quarta istruzione," 161–3.

The composition of local marriage rites seems to fall between a revision which maintains the substantial unity of the Roman Rite, and the more radical creativity required when attention is paid in liturgical inculturation to the rites and customs of peoples in entering marriage. On the one hand, the *Ordo Celebrandi Matrimonium* requires that the form of consent, the nuptial blessing, and the use of Scriptures follow the Roman ritual. On the other hand, its readiness to allow the development of a rite related to local marriage customs may represent quite a radical departure from what has become customary in the Roman Church, especially if these rites take place in homes and over a period of time.[55]

THE PROCESS AND METHODS OF LITURGICAL INCULTURATION

To offer a more comprehensive approach to liturgical inculturation suited to marriage ritual, the following discussion looks at the process and methodology of liturgical inculturation in different forms. For this we are particularly indebted to the work of Filipino liturgist Anscar Chupungco.

The Process of Inculturation

In speaking about process, the course an activity takes, the concern is "with what takes place between the *terminus a quo* or point of departure, and the *terminus ad quem* or point of arrival."[56] In liturgical inculturation the *terminus a quo* is provided by the Roman liturgical books and the people's cultural patterns. These two entities are made to interact, dialogue, and mutually animate each other, something which Chupungco compares to lighting a candle from both ends so that the light from each end meets in the center.[57] The *terminus ad quem*, the result or product of this process, is a new liturgy for the local Church.

We have already studied the newly revised Order for the Celebration of Marriage of the Roman Rite. Of equal importance is the cultural pattern which is at the other end of the *terminus a quo*. When people speak of cultural patterns they usually mean a people's typical mode of thinking, acting, speaking, and expressing themselves through rites, symbols, and art forms. A people's cultural pattern is their prescribed system of reflecting on, verbalizing, and ritualizing their values, traditions, and experiences. Cultural patterns are so cen-

[55] See Chapter I above, 16–20.
[56] Chupungco, *Liturgical Inculturation*, 32.
[57] Ibid.

tral and crucial that they influence society's values, ideologies, social and family traditions, and socioeconomic and political structures.[58] If cultural pattern, therefore, cuts across everything that constitutes the life of a society, it has to be given a principal role in the process of liturgical inculturation. The other argument for the essential place of culture and the need to respect cultural patterns in this task is the concrete experience of many a local church. Quite often people are dissatisfied with a liturgy that is foreign to their cultural pattern, and the risk is that such a liturgy only remains at the margins of their religious life. For "an inculturated liturgy is one whose shape, language, rites, symbols, and artistic expressions reflect the cultural pattern of the local Church."[59] Anything short of this is to risk becoming irrelevant or facing "the embarrassment of an overstaying alien."[60]

The Methods of Liturgical Inculturation

Chupungco identifies three methods which seem to have been successfully employed by the Church in the past: dynamic equivalence, creative assimilation, and organic progression. The effectiveness of these methods, he hastens to add, is relative to a number of factors. One is the prevailing theological reflection. This affects the choice and application of the method used. Another is the presence in a local church of a culture that "pulsates with life and vigor." Finally, the pastoral needs of the worshiping community dictate which method is most appropriate.[61] The ensuing discussion will describe the three different methods mentioned above.

THE METHOD OF DYNAMIC EQUIVALENCE

To denote the process whereby the Roman Rite is "translated" into other patterns of thought, language, and rites, Chupungco employs the term "dynamic equivalence." In essence, dynamic equivalence consists in replacing elements of the Roman liturgy with something in the local culture that has equal meaning or value.[62] The desired result

[58] The study of specific marriage customs, traditions, and beliefs is offered later in this book.

[59] Chupungco, *Liturgical Inculturation*, 37.

[60] Anscar Chupungco, *Cultural Adaptation of the Liturgy* (New York: Paulist Press, 1982) 58.

[61] Ibid.

[62] Anscar Chupungco, "Popular Religiosity and Liturgical Inculturation," *Ecclesia Orans* 8 (1991) 111; Chupungco, *Liturgical Inculturation*, 37.

in such a process is a liturgy whose language, rites, and symbols relate and resonate with the worshiping community's experiences, values, and traditions.

By its nature, dynamic equivalence is dependent on the typical edition of the liturgical books as a basis. These books are studied in their historical, pastoral, cultural, and theological contexts in order to determine which of their linguistic and ritual components may be replaced with equivalent native elements. This ensures the safeguarding of the liturgical tradition contained in the Roman Rite while it is being enriched and integrated with the culture of the people.[63] Although dynamic equivalence consists in replacing elements of the liturgy, it must be borne in mind that not everything may be replaced. At this point it is perhaps apropos to recall what *Sacrosanctum Concilium* 21 says and is repeated in the *Instruction on Inculturation:* "the liturgy is made up of immutable elements, divinely instituted, and of elements subject to change." To avoid any undiscerning or arbitrary application of the method, Chupungco outlines two preliminary steps. The first calls for the identification of the theological content of a rite, neatly distinguishing it from its liturgical form; the second calls for isolating the immutable elements from the elements which are subject to change.[64]

The theological content is the meaning of the liturgical text or rite. Basically it is the paschal mystery present in various degrees and under different aspects in the celebration since every liturgical rite contains, signifies, and celebrates this central mystery of our salvation. It is only expressed in various ritual forms according to the meaning and purpose of each rite. The liturgical form is the ritual shape with which the theological content is visibly expressed in terms of ritual acts, gestures, and formularies.[65]

---

[63] Anscar Chupungco, *Liturgies of the Future: The Process and Methods of Inculturation* (Mahwah, N.J.: Paulist Press, 1989) 36.

[64] Ibid., 40. Such a process, however, seems easier said than done. It is not always easy to make the neat distinction between the content or essence and the forms, and between the immutable and changeable elements in the liturgy, which Chupungco suggests. Besides, this language of content vs. form can imply that the form is somewhat insignificant. For some critique of this method see Margaret Mary Kelleher's article "Issues in Inculturation: A Review Essay," *The Living Light* 26 (1990) 327–37.

[65] Chupungco, *Liturgical Inculturation,* 41.

In regard to the second step, Chupungco provides us with a rather rigid principle to follow: "If the theological content or the liturgical form is of divine institution, it may not be replaced with another content or form that will modify the meaning originally intended by Christ."[66] Thus, in the case of baptism, the washing with water and the Trinitarian formula are the irreplaceable liturgical form of baptism. However, the manner of washing and of expressing the Trinitarian formula, provided the theological content is preserved, is within the realm of dynamic equivalence. We know that throughout history the Church has utilized not only one but a plurality of ways.

THE METHOD OF CREATIVE ASSIMILATION

As the term suggests, this method of inculturation consists in the "assimilation of pertinent rites and linguistic expressions, religious or otherwise, used by the contemporary society" by the liturgy.[67] This method played a very significant role in the formation of the liturgy during the patristic period. Rites of particular relevance borrowed from the socioreligious traditions of the period were invested with Christian meaning, often through the system of biblical typology. Most of these were appended to the rites themselves and served as explanatory parts which elaborated on the core of the liturgical rite. Among these borrowed rites, Chupungco cites baptismal anointing, the giving of the cup of milk and honey, and the washing of the feet of neophytes as classic examples from the baptismal liturgy of that period. These have been preserved in some contemporary rites such as the Ambrosian rite at Milan.

Nevertheless, in view of the provisions contained in *Sacrosanctum Concilium* 38–39 and 63b, creative assimilation should never be regarded as the ordinary method of liturgical inculturation. The mind of the council seems clear that the process of inculturation normally starts from the typical editions of the liturgical books. Surely, there are occasions when a fully renewed liturgy of a local church requires inculturation through the application of creative assimilation. But as the instruction *Comme le prévoit* stresses, "inculturation based on the typical editions is the best school and discipline for creativity in the liturgy."[68]

[66] Ibid., 42.
[67] Ibid., 44–5.
[68] Instruction *Comme le prévoit*, no. 43, DOL, 291. Also cited in Chupungco, *Liturgical Inculturation*, 46.

However, in some cases like marriage, funerals, and blessings, creative assimilation seems the only realistic method in the development of a particular ritual with respect to the culture, traditions, and life situation of a local church. Local churches can considerably enrich the typical editions of the rites by expanding their ritual shapes. In light of this, it would then be useful for these communities to look into the possibility of incorporating into the particular rituals suitable rites and symbols used in their own cultures and traditions. Through creative assimilation, these rituals will acquire a new shape, perhaps a new plan and a new set of rites and formularies. The notable thing about this process is that, unlike the method of dynamic equivalence, "the new features will not serve as dynamic equivalents [or replacements] of the elements present in the typical editions. They will act the part of protagonists in the elaboration of a new rite."[69]

THE METHOD OF ORGANIC PROGRESSION

Although inculturation normally should not depart from the provisions of the liturgical documents, it cannot operate exclusively within the text of the provisions. There are occasions or situations when the task of inculturation requires that the parameters set, explicitly or implicitly, by the liturgical documents be traversed. How to do this within the ambit of liturgical tradition and without doing violence to the true and authentic spirit of the liturgy is what the method of "organic progression" is all about.

Organic progression is described as "the work of supplementing and completing the shape of the liturgy established by the Constitution on the Liturgy and the *editio typica* of liturgical books."[70] This is accomplished by rereading these documents in the light of postconciliar experiences of the local churches with the objective of filling in what they lack or of putting to completion what they only partially or imperfectly state. Organic progression is "a way of saying that the new forms," which could evolve through this process, "should have been there all along, and that if the liturgical rite were drawn up today, they would surely be part of it."[71]

The method is "progressive" because of the new shape it gives to liturgy. This is brought about by the dynamics of supplementation,

[69] Chupungco, *Liturgical Inculturation*, 46.

[70] Anscar Chupungco, "Inculturation and the Organic Progression of the Liturgy," *Ecclesia Orans* 7 (1990) 9.

[71] Ibid., 10; Chupungco, *Liturgical Inculturation*, 47.

whereby new elements are introduced into the liturgy, and continuance, which is a sequel to the work begun by the council and the Holy See. It is also "organic" because its result complies with the basic intention of the liturgical documents and, on a wider breath, with the nature and tradition of Christian worship.[72] In light of the foregoing one can say with Chupungco that:

"Organic progression is not a work of fantasy, but of creativity and inventiveness based on liturgical principles and tradition. If it results in something which has not been envisaged by the official documents, it is because no liturgical text is ever the final draft, because liturgical renewal will always remain an unfinished agenda."[73]

Organic progression is implied in *Sacrosanctum Concilium* 23 which underlines that no innovations be made unless the good of the Church genuinely and certainly requires them, "and care must be taken that any new forms adapted should in some way grow organically from forms already existing." The phrase "new forms" may be taken to suggest that new rites can actually be created, albeit within the limits set by the conciliar provisions. Organic progression moves onward from where the Constitution on the Liturgy and the *editio typica* stop because the framers of both documents could not have foreseen every possible need of every local church. The presence of *lacunæ* especially in the typical editions is but a proof of the important role and task of local churches in the inculturation process. If it is deemed necessary these local churches may develop new ritual forms "organically progressing" from existing official forms. Although the *editio typica* of the liturgical books normally offer a wide range of options and possibilities, the breadth of inculturation should not be hemmed in by the provisions contained by the document.[74] Moreover, typical editions cannot possibly envisage all the options and possibilities for inculturation which should be made available to the local churches.

In a sense, therefore, organic progression, as a contextual interpretation of liturgical documents, is a continuation of the work of the council and the Holy See. It works with the conviction that the present phase of liturgical reform is short of being final or definitive and

---

[72] Chupungco, "Inculturation and the Organic Progression of the Liturgy," 9.
[73] Ibid.
[74] Chupungco, *Liturgical Inculturation*, 50.

that in order to realize the liturgical renewal envisioned by Vatican II the work of development, the filling of the *lacunæ*, must proceed.

The Church is actually no stranger to organic progression. There have been times when it used this method in responding to pastoral needs. To illustrate this Chupungco supplies the following examples: the use of the vernacular in all liturgical celebrations; the incorporation of new elements into the typical editions, like general absolution and new eucharistic prayers; the faculty to repeat anointing in the course of the same illness; the permission to use another kind of plant oil for the sacrament of the sick; and the possibility of drawing up particular orders of the Mass.[75]

In the context of particular cultures, it is difficult to speak of one single method best suited for the work. The principles of inculturation, and the richness and peculiarity of a culture's marriage practices and beliefs, demand some use of all three methods. When it comes to the more radical adaptations mentioned in the Vatican Constitution on the Liturgy, besides the methods presented by Chupungco a way of considering the total context is also necessary. Hence we proceed now to what is currently called the contextualization of faith and its expressions.

THE METHOD OF CONTEXTUALIZATION

A creative approach to liturgical inculturation may benefit from what has often been referred to as the method of inculturation. As presented even by Chupungco, the method of inculturation does seem to be quite limited in its treatment of culture.[76] Interest seems to be confined to a formal consideration of human experience, that is, to cultural values, beliefs, customs, and rituals, and popular religiosity but pays very little attention, if any, to other aspects of the total historical context of a people. Contextualization, on the contrary, is a term that is wider in scope. It includes the realities of contemporary secularity, technology, social change, economic and political realities, and the struggle for human justice and liberation. It thus broadens the understanding of culture and looks at culture in more dynamic and

[75] Ibid.
[76] Actually, Chupungco himself includes a rather brief treatment of contextualization in his book *Liturgical Inculturation*. He sees it as a part of the inculturation process. He is of the opinion that although contextualization involves the interaction between liturgy and culture, it is directly concerned with the situation of repression and deprivation. Hence, contextualization is oftentimes identified with the agenda of liberation theology. See Chupungco, *Liturgical Inculturation*, 19–21.

flexible ways, not as self-contained but as an open entity capable of being enriched and modified through mutual exchanges with other cultures. Contextualization likewise includes the need to respect and deal with previous forms of theology and Christian practice that, while not native to culture, have over the years become part of it.[77] In other words, it takes into consideration the total historical context of a specific culture or people in their particularity.

Contextualization: A Brief Description

Albeit understood and interpreted in various ways, authors basically agree that contextualization is a process "aimed at making the different forms of Christian expression relevant to the societal contexts where they occur."[78] As an activity by which a local church integrates the Gospel message (the text) into its own culture (the context),[79] it calls for the expression of Christian thought and praxis in terms of the thought forms, language, and symbols of particular cultures. It likewise involves the task of relating the Christian message to the concrete life expressions and situation of the people. Here, however, we do not want to cover the whole range of literature dealing with contextualization. We want to see it as done in the context of the Filipino peoples. Hence we begin with the way in which the method is described by Stephen Bevans. Bevans is an American, a Divine Word Missionary, who taught theology for many years in the region of the Philippines known as the Ilocos. It was there that he began to develop the approach which he describes in his book, *Methods of Contextual Theology*. Along with the work of Bevans, attention will be given to the theology of the Filipino writers José de Mesa, Dionisio Miranda, and Leonardo Mercado. While these writers have the Philippines in mind, their work can apply in many parts of the world, especially for

[77] Stephen Bevans, *Models of Contextual Theology* (Maryknoll, N.Y.: Orbis Books, 1992) 21.

[78] Justin Ukpong, "Contextualization: Concept and History," *Revue Africaine de Théologie* 2 (1987) 152. Parallel to Chupungco's concept of "adaptation," Ukpong takes "contextualization" as the umbrella term embracing all forms of endeavor with the purpose of making the dialogue or encounter between the Judeo-Christian tradition and other cultures possible, i.e., indigenization, inculturation, translation, and others.

[79] Louis Luzbetak, *The Church and Cultures: New Perspectives in Missiology* (Maryknoll, N.Y.: Orbis Books, 1988) 69. In this book the author understands contextualization as synonymous with incarnation and inculturation.

peoples in the process of post-colonial cultural, social, and political retrieval.

Bevans describes contextualization as:

"a way of doing theology in which one takes into account: the spirit and message of the *gospel;* the *tradition* of the Christian people; the culture in which one is theologizing; and *social change* in that culture, whether brought about by western technological process or the grassroots struggle for equality, justice and liberation."[80]

Contextualization stands in sharp contrast to the "classical" approach in theology which understood itself as an objective science of faith with Scripture and tradition as the almost exclusive sources for reflection. What makes theology or liturgy contextual is precisely the acknowledgment of the validity of another *locus theologicus:* present human experience.[81] It recognizes that apart from Scripture and tradition, culture, culture change, history, and contemporary thought forms are legitimate sources for theological reflection and expression. This flows from the conviction that our cultural and historical context plays a part in the construction of the reality in which we live and which inescapably molds and influences our understanding of God and the ways we express our faith and belief.[82]

Contextualization is a task and process of making the Gospel message and the liturgy meaningful and challenging in specific cultural contexts. This is not merely a matter of expressing the Christian faith or Christian liturgy in culturally intelligible categories, although this is an essential component. It must also respond to the actual challenges of the situation, the real and present context wherein the local church finds itself.[83] If our theology and liturgy are to make sense, that is, to be relevant, reasonably comprehensible, and meaningful for

[80] Bevans, *Models of Contextual Theology*, 1. Italics are mine.

[81] Ibid., 2. Human experience and culture are used interchangeably by Bevans in as much as whenever we speak of human experiences we are, in fact, referring to culturally defined experiences. This becomes clear when we recall Geertz' concept of culture as "webs of significance," as a set of meanings that informs a people's way of life, or as the organized system of knowledge, customs, beliefs, and symbols whereby a community structures its experiences and perceptions.

[82] "Reality," writes Bevans, "is mediated by meaning, a meaning we give it in the context of our culture or our historical period, interpreted from our own particular horizon and in our particular thought forms." Ibid.

[83] José de Mesa, *In Solidarity with the Culture* (Quezon City: Maryhill School of Theology, 1987) 4. The title of the first chapter of this book seems to indicate that

people of today, they have to immerse themselves in the present-day realities of suffering, oppression, and to search for that liberating word spoken by God within the experience of the poor and the oppressed of this world.[84] Preparing a meaningful liturgy, therefore, demands that we keep in mind the particular situation, with its changing culture, popular or folk religiosity, the socioeconomic and political realities which the people confront or live with from day to day, as well as the issues of justice and the struggle for total human development or liberation.

In elaborating on the inculturation of the Gospel, Filipino ethicist Dionisio Miranda distinguishes between indigenization and contextualization.[85] He defines indigenization as a process of inculturation which is focused on the "'substantive,' the 'constitutive,' or 'structural' emics of a particular culture."[86] On the other hand, the work of inculturation can be called contextualization in as much as it refers to "a process wherein the emphasis is on the 'processual,' 'developmental,' or 'generative' emics of culture."[87] Miranda finds that this allows for attention to the creative change that occurs in culture within changing temporal and historical circumstances. As he notes, such change occurs in the renewal of the structures of life and the redirection of mentalities to meet the demands of modernity. In the inculturation of the Gospel, the Church has to attend to both processes, that is, to the task of discovering the enduring meanings and values of a culture, and to that of seeing how culture changes in the face of changing circumstances.

The distinction made by Miranda is useful insofar as it makes the point that culture needs to be studied in its historical and social conditions, and that it evolves as the conditions of a people's lives

---

de Mesa himself prefers calling this theological process inculturation rather than contextualization, but what he does corresponds to what Bevans calls contextualization. For reasons already given above on pages 93–4 this writer prefers the term contextualization.

[84] José de Mesa and L. Wostyn, *Doing Theology* (Quezon City: Claretian Publications, 1990) 3–4.

[85] Dionisio M. Miranda, "Outlines of a Method of Inculturation," *East Asian Pastoral Review* 30 (1993) 145–67. See also his book *Buting Pinoy: Probe Essays on Value as Filipino* (Manila: Logos Publications, 1992) 227–33.

[86] Miranda, "Outlines of a Method," 148. The word *emics* is taken from linguistics to refer to the analysis of the elements found in cultures, which are comparable to the phonemes found in a language.

[87] Ibid., 153.

change. However, Miranda uses it in a rather static way by contrasting a people's "essential identity" with their "existential identity."[88] In other words, he believes that indigenization discovers essential and permanent meanings and values in a culture, which are then over the course of time transposed into varying contexts. The reality and evolution of a culture seem in fact to be more dynamic, and more inextricably bound with historical reality and social structure. A better approach, therefore, is to see contextualization as the key dynamic both in the heritage of culture itself and in the bringing of the Gospel or of Christian liturgy to a culture. It is always within a given set of historical, familial, social, and economic structures and conditions that a people retrieves its memories, embeds its symbols and rituals, redefines its familial kinships, and appropriates them into the developing horizons of a worldview.

In his book *Christ in the Philippines*, systematic theologian Leonardo Mercado expresses a preference for the term "contextualization" over "inculturation." This is because "it does not only embrace traditional culture but also 'takes into account the process of secularity, technology, and the struggle for human justice, which characterizes the historical movement in the Third World.'"[89] When Mercado appeals to the model of the incarnation for an inculturated theology, he gives importance to the action of contextualizing faith in Christ, and the image of Christ proclaimed to the Filipino people. He also notes that the people themselves have to be seen as the primary agents of contextualization.[90] It is they who in their faith and customs and in their way of speaking relate belief in Christ to their own world. In his later writings, however, he appears to give more preference for the term "inculturation" over "contextualization," without substantially altering his approach.[91]

Bevans places both Mercado and Miranda among contextual theologians, giving their method the more precise designation of anthro-

---

[88] Ibid., 154. His approach seems to be restricted by his subscription to and reliance on the substance/accident dichotomy of Western philosophy.

[89] Leonardo N. Mercado, *Christ in the Philippines* (Tacloban City: Divine Word University Publications, 1982) 19. Mercado here cites Douglas J. Elwood, *What Asian Christians Think: A Theological Source Book* (Quezon City: New Day Publishers, 1976) 48.

[90] Mercado, *Christ in the Philippines*, 24–6.

[91] See for example, Leonardo Mercado, *Inculturation and Filipino Theology* (Manila: Divine Word Publications, 1992); Leonardo Mercado, *Doing Filipino Theology* (Manila: Divine Word Publications, 1997).

pological model.[92] This is because they both take human experience, as expressed in Filipino cultures, as their theological starting point. In this they are contrasted with another contextualist, José de Mesa, to whose work we now turn.

Culture, Cultural Change, and Identity[93]

There is no question that culture shapes a people's way of acting and thinking, providing, as it does, models of reality which govern perception. To understand the experiences of a people one must learn about their culture, since experiences are always interpreted from a specific cultural frame of reference. Cultures fashion perceptions of reality or experiences into conceptualizations of what reality can or should be, what is considered as actual, possible, or impossible. These conceptualizations form the worldview of a culture, to which members consciously or unconsciously assent. Worldview lies at the core of a culture, for it is from this that a people's value system and standards of judgment and conduct originate. Therefore culture, as an integrated system of beliefs, values, customs, and of institutions expressing these beliefs, customs, and values, serves to bind a community together and gives it a sense of identity, security, and continuity.[94]

Culture, however, is not a static reality. Culture can and does change because it is historically situated. While culture shapes and conditions people, it is people themselves who create culture. Through their experiences they do not only create and preserve culture but also modify and change it. And with the change in culture and cultural patterns the network of meanings, the perception of reality, and the worldview are also modified. With cultural change the identity, security, and continuity of a people and their way of life is also disturbed.

In the context of the Filipino experience, the issue of culture and cultural change is particularly significant for at least two reasons: the

[92] Bevans, *Models of Contextual Theology,* 51–2.
[93] I present here only the salient points in de Mesa's discussion of the subject. See de Mesa and Wostyn, *Doing Theology,* 24–30. In the range of models which he includes under the umbrella of contextual theology, Bevans places the work of de Mesa within the compass of synthetic models that establish a dialogue between culture and the Christian tradition. Bevans, *Models of Contextual Theology,* 92–6.
[94] Here de Mesa quotes what he refers to as the Willowbank Report (1978) for this definition of culture. See de Mesa and Wostyn, *Doing Theology,* 25. No further information on this report is supplied.

present experience of modernization and globalization and, more importantly, the cultural imbalances brought about by the two successive waves of colonization; namely, that of Spain and the United States. A brief explanation can be given of each.

To borrow Marshal McLuhan's words, modernization, with its digital technology that provides almost unlimited access to the information superhighway, has reduced the world into a global village. This has accelerated the process of transformation of many societies, their customs, traditions, values, beliefs, and institutions. Contextual theology takes into consideration all these changes. It does not base itself solely on a fossilized culture of a bygone era which no longer exists, such as the pre-colonial times. Comparisons and contrasts are helpful, but strictly speaking theological reflection concentrates more on the people's present cultural experience, always remembering that cultures are consistently in flux, ever in the process of becoming, adapting, and changing.

In parts of the world, such as the Philippines, colonization and westernization have produced an overall effect of disequilibrium so that the traditional balance of the indigenous society has been upset.[95] This disequilibrium has precipitated social and cultural changes. It has brought people to a difficult period of transition from an indigenous way of life to one that has been greatly westernized. Westernization, it must be admitted, has not been entirely negative. Nonetheless, while Ilocanos seem to have imbibed a lot of their colonizers' values, the evidence is far too clear that they are not quite at home in their "western garb." Among other things, colonization had led to the depreciation of the native culture and consequently of the dignity of the native peoples.[96] Cultural, political, and economic subjugation has fostered a feeling of inferiority among the colonized. It generated a perception among them that anything indigenous is of poorer quality or second class, and that anything from the colonizing country is always better. A contextualized theology and liturgy are needed to help the people search for their identity, to bring them to a new consciousness of their self-worth and independence. This process will facilitate the rediscovery of the riches and potential of their culture that have been obscured by their colonial experience. This theological method will lead them to appreciate the inherent goodness of many of their

[95] De Mesa, and Wostyn, *Doing Theology,* 29.
[96] De Mesa, *In Solidarity with the Culture,* 11.

values which are just as good, if not better than, those of their past masters. Only such will enable the subjugated "to find themselves, reestablish continuity with their own past history and culture, gain status in their own eyes as a distinct people, and re-evaluate their achievements and potentialities in view of the future."[97]

It is indeed imperative to emphasize the retrieval of positive cultural resources and potential of every local Church which may have been eclipsed and obscured by the process of westernization or which may be gradually disappearing and disintegrating in the wake of modernization. Naturally, these will be modified in their expression when taken into a contemporary context. But it is important to see them as part of a rich cultural heritage. In order that this does not degenerate into a form of cultural romanticism, it has to have a critical component. It must also unmask and critique the death-dealing elements present in the culture, the negative values and structures which spawn bad habits, vices, and sinfulness that are detrimental to total human development and the enjoyment of the fullness of life promised by Jesus.

Socioeconomic and Political Realities[98]

A meaningful theology or liturgy ought to respond to the actual challenges of the total situation in which the local church finds itself. It has to confront not only the issue of cultural identity but also other pressing questions such as justice and liberation in the context of the socioeconomic and political realities within which people live. In proclaiming the Good News, the promise and reality of life in Jesus, it must address the total historical context, the life and death situation of the people in all aspects of their day to day struggles.

Contextualizing theological reflection and liturgical worship will often mean that we take account of the fact that many people live below the poverty line, since wealth and access to the benefits of development are controlled by a favored few. It needs to take cognizance of the lack of a sense of stewardship of the earth's resources, of ecological degradation at the guise of the so-called development

[97] De Mesa and Wostyn, *Doing Theology*, 30.

[98] The bigger picture of the Philippine situation can be found in Appendix I of the *Acts and Decrees of the Second Plenary Council of the Philippines*, 20 January–17 February 1991 (Manila: Catholic Bishops' Conference of the Philippines, 1992). See also National Conference of Catholic Bishops, "Pastoral Letter, 25 January 1999," *Weltkirche* 22 (1999) 43–54.

whose benefits only slowly and minimally trickle down to the poor. It has to take into consideration the reality in certain regions of political dynasties, of the unholy alliance between political power and economic wealth, where politics is the weapon often used to protect and promote the vested interests of the privileged few at the expense of the common good.

In a situation where people live in seeming helplessness, hopelessness, and despair because of their apparent powerlessness within these prevailing socioeconomic and political structures, there is a need for a theology and liturgy that enables people to discover the liberating Word of God that allows them to hope amidst poverty, suffering, and oppression. A truly contextualized theology and liturgy could lead people to an experience, albeit partial, of the fullness of life, the total salvation and liberation which God offers by empowering them to unearth the resources found in the Judeo-Christian tradition and their own culture so that they can effectively bring about change in their own situation. What we need is a theology and liturgy that proclaim and celebrate human dignity, our unity, equality, and freedom as children of God, our unity and responsibility for one another and the whole of creation. We want a theology and liturgy that challenge the systems, ideologies, and structures that perpetuate oppression and discrimination and which facilitate the people's empowerment through a recovery of their identity, retrieval of their positive sociocultural and religious values, so that they too can discover and celebrate the active presence of God in their lives.

Popular Religiosity

To a great extent, it is through popular religiosity that we are, as Mercado states it, provided with the model of "people-as-contextualizer."[99] An instance of this is seen in the incorporation by the people of the stories, symbols, and rituals of their cultural inheritance into the rituals and liturgy of marriage. In this people find not only their traditional beliefs and perspectives, but also their way of relating a Christian vision and practice of marriage to this inheritance.

Sometimes referred to as "folk Catholicism," popular religiosity may be described as the peculiar manner in which Filipinos and other peoples have integrated their Catholic beliefs and practices with their native ways of thinking and acting, their particular ways of believing

[99] Mercado, *Christ in the Philippines*, 24–6.

and worshiping. In practice this is manifested in their overt acceptance of normative or official Catholic doctrine and ritual, while at the same time, in their concrete religious behavior, their activities are heavily oriented toward the observances of popular beliefs and practices sanctioned by the community but not necessarily by the official Church hierarchy.[100] This has involved the modification of the official doctrines, rituals, and practices in order to accommodate local needs. The people, in accepting these religious elements from the West, have given them cultural form by endowing them with ceremonial and emotional content, thus making them their own. Popular religiosity, with its wealth of symbols and expressions, can help creatively transform the official liturgy into a more dynamic and more meaningful form of worship.

Nevertheless, contextual theology must also explore the need to purify popular religiosity and its many manifestations of its various damaging dimensions. As a positive or faith-response to divine revelation, it is fundamentally good. But because it is embodied in a local culture, hence sharing in its strengths and weaknesses, discernment is needed. Popular religiosity should be evaluated in terms of its life-giving and death-dealing elements.[101] In addition, there is also the task of investigating the claim that the reason popular religiosity remains strong even after centuries of Catholicism is inadequate evangelization and insufficient faith formation. Popular religiosity or folk Catholicism might well be criticized for an emphasis on external practices rather than on the deeper meaning of the mysteries of God as they impact on daily life. It has to be critiqued for its contribution in fostering the so-called split-level Christianity or the dichotomy between faith and life among Ilocano Christians. Furthermore, as theological reflection focuses on how popular religiosity can be expanded and balanced by the Scriptures and Christian tradition, its contribution to a more contextualized, more meaningful liturgy can also be examined.

Inserted into a method of contextualization, the richness of a study of popular religiosity emerges in several ways. First, it is largely through it that the traditional beliefs, symbols, and rites have remained a part of the life of peoples. Second, it has served to relate

[100] Victor Maynigo, "Evangelization and Philippine Culture in the Light of the Second Vatican Council" (S.T.D. dissertation, Pontifical University of St. Thomas, Rome, 1978) 22.

[101] De Mesa and Wostyn, *Doing Theology*, 33.

Christianity to the cultural, social, and economic life of the people, and expresses resistance to foreign imposition. Third, amidst the changes imposed by colonization it has kept alive the relationship of the people to the land and to kin, and has maintained an equality and mutuality between man and woman in relationships and public roles which were not given due respect by missionaries. Finally, a critique of popular religiosity in face of its resistance to social change shows how beliefs and customs, however traditional, have to change and adapt amidst newly emerging social and economic situations.

BASIC THEOLOGICAL ORIENTATION

While in one sense contextualization may be said to take its inspiration from the incarnational nature of Christianity, it can also be said to have a basic theological orientation that is "creation-centered." In this sense its proponents see it as closely related to Rahner's theology of God's self-communication in creation which is brought to fullness in Christ.[102] This orientation is "characterized by the conviction that culture and human experience are generally good. Its perspective is that grace builds on nature, but only because nature is capable of being built on, of being perfected in a supernatural relationship with God."[103] Underlying this conviction is the belief in the "sacramental" nature of reality. The ordinary things and events of life are transparent of God's presence. In and through our human experiences, God continues to offer us a full and meaningful life amidst our struggles to find and create meaning in a world of suffering and oppression. In our world and through concrete things, we continue to encounter God in Jesus. If this is indeed true, then one can speak of culture and events in history, of "contexts," as truly sacramental, and hence revelatory.[104]

Contextualization affirms that God's revelation or offer of life and love happens in and through human experiences in the cultural world, in our ordinary situations. The human experiences in our historical and cultural settings are the very same experiences which mediate God's gift of total salvation, albeit in a provisional and fragmentary manner. It is precisely in our history, the pattern of human experiences, that salvation (already but not yet) is concretely

[102] See for example, Karl Rahner, *Foundations of Christian Faith*, trans. William Dych (New York: Seabury Press, 1978) 138–46.
[103] Ibid., 16.
[104] Ibid., 8–9.

experienced.[105] Without ignoring the reality of imperfection and sin in culture and history, contextualization sees a continuity between human existence and divine reality. "Revelation and human experience are inseparable aspects of a single event: that of the disclosure of God to human beings who recognize and freely accept such manifestations."[106] For in the very setting we find ourselves as individual persons, members of a specific culture, class, or group at a particular space and time, we can experience God. God reveals Godself in the historical realities in which we are immersed. As de Mesa puts it so plainly and straightforwardly:

"Our salvation history is not found in the Holy land; it is found in our own land and in our own people's history. Our lands are holy because in these very lands God is present; our histories are histories of salvation because God is at work in and through them offering us life and love."[107]

A SKETCH OF THE PROCESS

The theological method which de Mesa proposes claims to guarantee a theological reflection that is both meaningful and relevant to contemporary Christians. Essentially, it consists of a dialectical and critical reading together or mutual interaction of the two poles of the theological enterprise: the pole of the Judeo-Christian tradition and the pole of our present-day experience, located within a specific cultural and historical matrix.[108]

Stages of the Process

The methodology in contextualization consists in a critical correlation of the two poles of theological reflection which begins with the contemporary human experiences of a people within a specific situation or culture, and then confronts the questions and issues emerging from it in the light of the Gospel or the Judeo-Christian tradition.

De Mesa describes the methodological procedure in three stages.[109] In the first stage, the total human situation is addressed, bringing to attention the issues, questions, and concerns that arise from the

[105] Jose de Mesa, *Following the Way of the Disciples* (Quezon City: East Asian Pastoral Institute, 1996) 21.

[106] De Mesa and Wostyn, *Doing Theology,* 72.

[107] De Mesa, *Following the Way of the Disciples,* 22.

[108] De Mesa and Wostyn, *Doing Theology,* 17.

[109] See ibid., 15–22 for a brief description of the process.

socioeconomic, cultural, political, and religious dimensions. With a respectful attitude the positive resources and potential of the culture are unearthed through some form of cultural analysis. Attention is to be focused on those aspects or elements of the native culture which have or can have a bearing on the situation or issue.

In the second stage, the cultural aspects or elements identified in the first are critically but responsibly correlated with the Judeo-Christian tradition. The relevant cultural aspects serve as interpretative elements (hence as source) in discerning and discovering the wealth and power of the Judeo-Christian tradition relative to the present context or situation. The rediscovery or retrieval of cultural resources leads to a further discovery which is that of the relevance of the Judeo-Christian tradition in the contemporary situation. Through this hermeneutical process the Gospel or the Christian message becomes more meaningful to the people as their understanding of it is deepened and intensified. The other side of the equation is that of the Judeo-Christian tradition interpreting, in a critical yet respectful stance, the relevant aspects of the indigenous culture. The tradition also throws light on the native culture, enabling the theologian and liturgist to discover the riches and strengths of the culture. This process contributes to the enhancement of the cultural identity of a people.

While the emphasis is on the rediscovery and retrieval of positive elements of the local culture, the critical component of this methodology also sees to the unmasking of the negative aspects. The Judeo-Christian tradition functions as a tool for discernment, challenging the limitations and weaknesses of a particular culture. Tradition cautions us to the dimensions and elements of the indigenous culture that inhibit the truth of the Gospel from getting incarnated in the lives of the people.

The third stage is the tentative and provisional result of the critical and respectful interaction between the two poles. The outcome of this dialogue is a culturally intelligible theological interpretation or a culturally intelligible liturgy (liturgical rite) which addresses the issues, questions, and concerns that stimulated the theological process in the first place. Stress is made on the "tentative" character of the theological reflection or the liturgy (liturgical rite) because it is never meant to be the final or definitive answer to the questions or issues raised. The fruits of theological reflection are meant to have an impact on the situation, thereby effecting change. Moreover, the theological process is an ongoing activity because the human situation which is ever-changing calls for an ongoing faith reflection as well. Every new situation and experience necessitates a fresh theological reflection and interpretation. Hence the image that could best illustrate the method of contextualization is not a hermeneutical circle but a spiral.[110]

Preparing a Contextualized Ilocano Liturgy of Marriage

Having described at length a method of contextualization, its guiding principles, and the processes involved, let us now look at how this might be applied in the preparation of a contextualized liturgy of marriage.

From a strictly liturgical point of view, the more immediate task in contextualization is for each local church to study its own culture and identify the elements which need to be retrieved, after being subjected to respectful yet critical appraisal, in shaping a liturgy that is both reflective of their own culture and faithful to the Judeo-Christian tradition. In this way, the divinely instituted or most basic elements of Christian liturgy remain, but the forms may vary from one local church to another and are not monolithic or uniform.[111]

We have seen how the 1991 *Ordo Celebrandi Matrimonium* allows for the development of a rite related to local marriage customs and traditions, especially if these indigenous rites take place in the homes and over a period of time. With this is the "minimum requirement" that the consent of the parties be asked for and obtained by the ordained minister or assisting layperson, that the nuptial blessing be given, and that Scriptures be used.[112]

In preparing a contextualized liturgy of marriage it is important to identify the positive aspects of the local culture relative to marriage. Having identified some of these expressions and values, they can be subjected to the critical hermeneutic of the Judeo-Christian tradition to find out if they may serve as authentic sources, components, or expressions of the Christian mystery.

Some points will be mentioned here that are pertinent to the peoples of the Philippines but which also play a role in other cultural

[110] This could be compared with the stages outlined by Leonardo Mercado, *Inculturation and Filipino Theology* (Manila: Divine Word Publications, 1992) 18–39. Cf. Leonardo Mercado, *Christ in the Philippines* (Tacloban City: Divine Word University Publications, 1982) 3–26; Leonardo Mercado, *Doing Filipino Theology* (Manila: Divine Word Publications, 1997) 3–19. As noted earlier, Mercado's vocabulary oscillates between preference for inculturation and preference for contextualization.

[111] A more thorough discussion of theological content and forms was presented above on the method of dynamic equivalence.

[112] See ROCM nos. 39–44.

traditions, especially where non-Western values and behaviors are at work, some perhaps that predate the era of colonization.

Extended Celebrations of Marriages

In some regions of the Philippines, from pre-colonial times up to our own day, marriage has been celebrated as a process, as an event ritualized in different stages and in varied settings. There are prenuptial negotiations and preparations which are accompanied by ritual. In the Philippines, the celebration reaches its highpoint in the exchange of vows at the liturgy of marriage in church where other explanatory rites adapted from the Mozarabic rite have been added to the Roman Rite. The ceremonies continue at the place of reception, usually at the home of either the bride or groom, and extends until the day after the wedding. Throughout the celebrations significant rituals are performed that bespeak of the people's view of marriage and the relationships now forged.

The extended celebration, beginning with a form of betrothal, provides the space for a young couple to be initiated into the ways and responsibilities of married life and into the forging of a union with each other that is not the matter of an instant but takes time to make. The rituals that could take place between the time of betrothal and the time of marriage guide them along the way. The rituals that over several days mark the final entering into marriage express the nature of marital union and commitment, as well as the changing relation to the extended family and society of a married couple. As has been noted by the Roman order of marriage celebration itself, where this is a custom, the ritual configuration must include the domestic rites before and after the marriage rites in the church. These rites of passage and celebration are very helpful to those entering such a union and taking on its commitments. In our days, when marriage stability is often threatened, the value of this extended preparation and domestic marriage ritual seems particularly pertinent.

Noting that the new order has provided a rite of engagement or betrothal, it is possible to turn to traditional cultures, as among the Ilocano people in the Philippines, to learn how it might be possible to construct a continuous rite or ritual process (a *ritus continuus*) that goes from the first engagement of a couple to the final ceremonies of marriage covenant. This is all the more important when the entire community is involved in the process and not only the couple or their immediate family.

To take one example that may stand for many cultural groups, the Ilocos and the Ilocanos have not been spared from the effects of modernization and cultural exchanges so that many of their indigenous customs and their meanings have been lost or have undergone some transformation or evolution in order to meet new needs or correspond to contemporary realities. Shaping a marriage rite must not lose sight of this, if it is to avoid falling into cultural romanticism. A rite should never impose customs and traditions which have fallen into disuse, especially when people can no longer acknowledge their significance.

Kinship and Family

Within this extended celebration, it is important to look into the culture's network of kinship and family relationships. In the Philippines, for example, a good number of rituals accompanying marriage are celebrated in the home by members of the families and clans of both parties. These celebrations with their rites and symbols underscore the cultural view of marriage, which is seen as more than merely an affair between husband and wife but as an event that involves their families and clans as well. This corresponds to situations in which the family is a source of identity and security where loyalty is very much valued. While membership in a family imposes certain obligations, it is in turn a steady source of support and assistance especially in times of need. The domestic rituals highlighting the role of the families in helping to assure the success of the marriage and the family they are going to build need to be incorporated into the marriage liturgy.

On the other hand, the hermeneutic of suspicion points to two risks in the importance given to kinship and family. The first is that kinship rituals may bear no reference to current familial and economic changes. Thus the challenge to ritual expression is to represent what may be the enduring bonds that keep people together in a shared inheritance of cultural values and affective ties, but in a different context of social and economic structures, where the modes of sharing are not necessarily the same as those of the past.

The second risk is that the larger family may be given priority over the commitment to Christ, the Church, and the reign of God. The Christian vision of marriage as a sacrament of the Church is one that can enrich, and sometimes challenge, the attachment of peoples to their family and kinship. It can also liberate them for the service of God's reign from the excessive demands of family, going outside the boundaries of the family and kinship in the service of others and the pursuit of their own vocation. Nonetheless, to symbolize both a marriage union and the nature of the Church as God's family, one can draw on the cultural sense of family that is found among some peoples. This understanding of family inherent to culture is rich and can fill out the notion of the Church as the family of God. At the same time, even while a couple are invited into the wider family of God, it cannot be ignored how much familial tradition and familial bonds are a part of a couple's identity. This identity can be corroded if this familial bonding and inheritance is not respected. Much that is truly compatible with or that comes from the Gospel is imbedded into people's lives through their adherence to their own cultural perspectives and worldview. To uproot such cultural inheritance threatens not only cultural identity but even true Gospel values that have been related to it by the people. On the other hand, it is true that a couple may at times be invited to give priority to their membership in the family of the Church over belonging to kin.

Giving and Exchanging of Gifts

The tradition of gift-giving is another notable feature of various cultures, where it is sometimes remarkably displayed on the occasion of marriages. Gifts offered and received on these occasions take on a sacred character and serve as tokens of commitment as well as to solidify personal relationships between individuals and families. The ritual of presenting and exchanging of gifts has long been a part of the Roman Rite of marriage, but only in the context of the rite celebrated in the church, as best exemplified in the exchange of rings. But when the celebration of marriage takes place in a series of stages from engagement to the day after the wedding celebration, it would be meaningful to integrate these gestures of gift-giving in a marriage rite that respects these stages and the accompanying domestic rituals. Amongst rural or fishing peoples, these gifts will often express a relationship of people to nature, and the rite of marriage should not lose this cosmic dimension. It need hardly be added that the accent on gift-giving coheres well with the Christian dispensation wherein we celebrate the great gift and wondrous exchange of the Incarnation and the abundance of the gifts of the Holy Spirit. Suitable prayer-texts may integrate the native sense of gift into the Christian understanding of sacrament as essentially God's self-giving, a giving mirrored in the spouses' mutual gift of self, as well as in the hospitality that a new home affords to others in the community.

However, in pursuit of the method of liturgical contextualization it has to be acknowledged that the exchange of gifts does not always take place in the same set of economic circumstances as in the past. In the past when families lived off the land their whole way of being was rooted in their oneness with nature and its rhythms. The exchange of gifts provided for subsistence as well as expressing the mutual love and interdependence of man and woman, or the pledge of parents and the larger family to the well-being of their children entering on marriage. Today, when a couple intends to live on the land and off the land amid their own kin, the symbol retains this meaning and practicality. Sometimes, however, the gift of land or of its produce may still be given to a newly married couple who will never live on this land. The relation to family and to nature that the gift expresses is therefore more tenuous. If the symbolic exchange is maintained, as it well may be, the ritual needs to express a relation to earth and the cosmos which people can maintain under new living conditions, and a relation to a cultural past and identity which may still nurture them in a different way of life.

Language

To form some idea of the role played by native language in the liturgy, we can turn to an example given in writing a contextualized moral theology. In developing a Filipino moral theology, the ethicist Dionisio Miranda roots his inquiry in linguistics.[113] He examines the Tagalog vocabulary of value, and from its analysis draws conclusions about the essential values of Filipino culture. He then critiques this in the light of Christian tradition, and finally looks for a Tagalog term that may best express a Christian sense of value that is grounded in this culture's own vocabulary. As Miranda employs it the approach may be too essentialist, but it highlights what is learned about a people through a study of its language. In the words of de Mesa: "It is not enough that the language utilized purports to relate to the experiences of the people; it must be a way of speaking which truly resonates with their experiences and, therefore, is experientially recognizable."[114]

In a comparable way, liturgy, to be truly rooted, needs a vocabulary that is drawn from the local culture, the familiar sphere of interhuman relationships and sociopolitical life. De Mesa argues that it is only

[113] Dionisio M. Miranda, "Fragments of a Method of Inculturation," *East Asian Pastoral Review* 30 (1993) 168–97.
[114] De Mesa and Wostyn, *Doing Theology*, 19.

when our theological and liturgical formulations are drawn from experience that we ensure their intelligibility. If this basic condition is not satisfied or if human experience is not expressed, the language used is bereft of meaning for the people.[115] Every culture has its own grammatical patterns, vocabulary and idioms, strengths and limitations, that need to be kept in mind in translating or composing liturgical texts. These will often have a bearing on marriage and family relations.

Theology of Marriage: Discipleship

In the Filipino context, de Mesa proposes that Christian marriage be seen as a way of discipleship.[116] He maintains that marriage is not a second-rate commitment but is as valuable and dignified as a life of virginity. To further argue that marriage is an authentic way of following Christ, he uses the image or model of covenant to symbolize both personal and social commitment. In this context marriage as discipleship implies a total, faithful, accepting, exclusive, and continuing commitment made in faith. This commitment is made not only to one's spouse but likewise to the children to be born through the marital union, and to the whole human family. It is a commitment as well to relational well-being. This fits well with the Ilocano vocabulary for marriage and with all that it signifies.

In spite of its usefulness, this model also has its limitations. For example, de Mesa in his presentation does not include a discussion on the importance of symbols, particularly those which have to do with the cosmic reality. Kinship and the family and its many implications in the life and relationships of a married couple were not given the attention they deserve. To provide a more complete and more balanced theology, therefore, these elements have to be given thoughtful consideration.

SUMMARY

This chapter has undertaken the task of presenting some theological and liturgical principles which might serve as guidelines in the work of shaping a liturgy of marriage for the Ilocos. First, we looked

[115] Ibid., 20.

[116] This thesis is developed in his book *Marriage Is Discipleship* (Quezon City: East Asian Pastoral Institute, 1995). De Mesa's discussion on this theme first appeared in two volumes of the East Asian Pastoral Review. See his articles "Marriage Is Discipleship 1," *East Asian Pastoral Review* 28 (1991) 313–96, and "Marriage Is Discipleship 2," *East Asian Pastoral Review* 29 (1992) 3–107.

into the 1994 Instruction, *The Roman Liturgy and Inculturation,* with an eye on what it says regarding the nature, principles, and procedures to be followed in liturgical inculturation. Then we considered Chupungco's ideas and proposals about liturgical inculturation. Since his methods do not exhaust all possibilities of liturgical cultural development, we next considered how the method of contextualization, as proposed by some Filipino writers, could be used in composing a marriage liturgy. Here we have given general principles. How these approaches work in practice will be illustrated in the example of the Ilocano people and the Ilocano liturgy which follows.

Chapter V

Investigating Ilocano Marriage Customs and Rites

What has already been said about the inculturation and contextualization of marriage liturgy can be illustrated by taking one concrete example. What has been chosen here is to consider the process that would be appropriate in that region of the Philippines called the Ilocos, and whose inhabitants are known as Ilocanos. In developing an Ilocano marriage liturgy, it is important to investigate Ilocano culture, especially its perspectives on marriage and the accompanying rituals.

The marriage customs of this region have developed over three distinct historical periods. There are still beliefs and practices that date back to the time before colonization by Spain in the sixteenth century, and so before the advent of Christian evangelization. Then there is the period during which there was a fusion of cultures and a strong Christian influence, since most of the people had been baptized into the Church. Finally, there is the contemporary age when marriage and family are much affected by new socioeconomic conditions that change ways of life, by the movement of peoples typical of the modern age, and by emigration from the region. With all of this, however, there goes a new cultural consciousness and a desire to retrieve even those pre-colonial cultural perspectives and values that mark a people's historical identity.

Before this examination of the link between culture and marriage can be undertaken, the tools needed have to be considered. After a brief historical overview, we will look at the possible contribution made by ethnography and ethnohistory.

A HISTORICAL OVERVIEW

Genuine appreciation of the Ilocano culture demands that it be viewed against the broader background of Philippine colonial history. For more than three centuries the Filipino nation was under Spanish hegemony so that by the end of the nineteenth century, all but a few institutions bore Hispanic features. By the middle of the twentieth century, however, what had been hispanized was americanized.[1] The over-all effect of this colonial experience has been the impoverishment and the bewilderment of the Filipino people as to their identity. Benigno Aquino once noted that because Spain and the United States have tried to remold the Filipinos "in their own image," which deprived them of their "soul," "they were an Asian people not Asian in the eyes of their fellow Asians, not Western in the eyes of the West."[2]

For our purposes here, greater attention will be given to Hispanic influence. Besides the fact that it was Spain which was instrumental in making the Philippines the only predominantly Catholic country in Southeast Asia, it was also the process of hispanization which was, for the most part, responsible for the marginalization of the once indigenous cultures of the natives.

The Spanish agenda in the Philippines during the sixteenth-century conquest was the radical transformation and reorganization of Filipino society. Whether the motive was primarily political or religious should not concern us here.[3] What is very clear, however, is the fact that the

[1] Heidi K. Gloria, "Ethnohistory, Ethnicity, and the Problem of Filipino Identity," *Tambara: The Ateneo de Davao University Journal* II (December 1985) 11. The Philippine Islands were discovered by the Spaniards in 1521 but the conquest did not begin until 1565. The archipelago was a colony of Spain until 1898 when the Americans took over. Sovereignty or political independence was granted to the nation on July 4, 1946. Philippine history has been neatly summed up as "three centuries in a Catholic convent and fifty years in Hollywood." See Stanley Karnow, *In Our Image: America's Empire in the Philippines* (New York: Ballantine Books, 1989) esp. 9.

[2] Benigno Aquino, "What's Wrong with the Philippines?" *Foreign Affairs* [no volume number given] (July 1968), quoted in Karnow, *In Our Image*, 25. Also quoted in Edmundo Valera, "Theology of Struggle: The Philippines' Ecclesial Experience," *New Theology Review* 5 (May 1992) 62.

[3] There are historians who claim that three objectives encouraged the Spaniards to colonize the Philippines: to secure a share in the lucrative spice trade which heretofore had been a Portuguese monopoly; to establish direct contact with China and Japan, which might pave the way for their conversion to Christianity; and to Christianize the inhabitants of the archipelago. See John Leddy Phelan, *The Hispanization of the Philippines: Spanish Aims and Filipino Responses* (Madison: University of Wisconsin Press, 1959) 4–6.

process of hispanization had its share of successes as well as failures. While it is true that the Filipino people owe their Christianity to the Spaniards, the methods of evangelization which were employed are not beyond criticism. Human as they were, the missionaries and conquerors, in their great zeal to "civilize" the natives and bring them into the light of the Gospel of Christ, were not always disposed to appreciate their indigenous cultural customs, beliefs, and ways.

The Filipino natives were no passive recipients of the cultural stimulus created by the conquest. They responded with considerable freedom, and their capacity for creative social and cultural adjustment is attested by the manner in which they adapted many Hispanic features to their own indigenous cultures.[4] More than anything else, it was the Spanish form of Christianity which facilitated the process of acculturation, to whose multiform appeal the Filipinos responded with much enthusiasm. The penchant for festivity and elaborate ritual and the devotion to the saints in Spanish Catholicism were readily accommodated to Filipino cultural perspectives.

The Ilocanos are no exception to this massive social and cultural transformation in the islands, for in a very short time they embraced the new religion. Conversion to Catholicism, however, had its own price. In the view of the Spaniards, their native anitistic religion[5] constituted the tyrannical enslavement of the devil. Therefore, for them to be liberated from the devil's oppressive sway the new converts had to abandon their "pagan" practices, traditions, and beliefs. Moreover, from the beginning the missionaries jealously guarded Christian worship lest contact with the people's "pagan" religion render it impure. Christianity was sealed against any cultural intrusion. Natives had to conform with the policy of deliberate rupture with their "pagan" past.

But as the Ilocano native culture is deeply embedded in the lives of the people, significant elements of the old anitistic religion blended into the new. As a result, the natives endowed certain aspects of the new religion with a special Ilocano flavor which made Catholicism in this region a unique expression of this universal religion. In other words, integration was more apparent than real so that it often resulted in religious syncretism.

---

[4] Ibid., viii.
[5] This will be explained below.

EARLY ILOCANO MARRIAGE RITUALS:
THE TASK OF ETHNOGRAPHY

Status Quaestionis

In addressing Ilocano marriage customs and beliefs, it is important to appreciate the significance of rituals and symbols in the lives of the people. If culture is to be understood as "webs of significance"[6] created by human persons, or as "essentially, a transmitted pattern of meanings embodied in symbols," then providing a description of the elements of Ilocano culture means entrance into the Ilocano's world of meaning. Therefore, when a foreign system of symbols is imposed on a people, its meaning-system inevitably gets disrupted. Consequently, it creates cultural ambivalence which at times tends dangerously toward cultural fragmentation,[7] resulting in the diminishment of the people's sense of identity and pride. This is the downside of Spanish evangelization in the Philippines.

Since part of the study is the attempt to reconstruct the religious life of the Filipino natives, particularly the Ilocanos, in the period before the advent of Christianity and the early Spanish times, historical materials constitute the primary sources. To accomplish this task we must employ "ethnohistory," the study of the history of peoples through the use of sources, both written and unwritten, with either diachronic or synchronic emphasis.[8] This is an approach that combines the historical method and some anthropological techniques.

---

[6] In Clifford Geertz's semiotic concept, culture is "a system of inherited conceptions expressed in symbolic forms by means of which human beings communicate, perpetuate and develop their knowledge about, and their attitudes towards life." It is a context within which events, behaviors, institutions, or processes can be intelligibly described. Geertz refers to this ethnographic task of making an intelligible account of the culture as necessarily interpretative or as "thick-description." This task, however, presupposes the ethnographer's immersion into the culture. See Clifford Geertz, *Interpretation of Cultures* (New York: Basic Books, 1973) 5–14.

[7] Gloria, "Ethnohistory, Ethnicity," 11.

[8] Ethnohistory has two principal interests. One is historical ethnography which is the reconstruction of a synchronic ethnographic description of a past stage of culture, especially a description based on written documents contemporary with this stage. The other is historiography of nonliterate cultures, which is the study and application of techniques of historical research such as the use of oral tradition, comparative ethnology, and archaeology. See William Sturtevant, "Anthropology, History, and Ethnohistory," *Introduction to Cultural Anthropology,* ed. James Clifton (Boston: Houghton Mifflin Company, 1968) 451–75.

A PROBLEMATIC TASK

To present a comprehensive ethnohistory, let alone a complete ethnography of Ilocano marriage customs, practices, and beliefs prior to the advent of the Gospel in the sixteenth century is a daunting task. More serious a problem than the lack of systematic and exhaustive studies is the dearth of materials dealing with them. The earliest descriptions of the Philippine Islands are the Chinese accounts of the thirteenth and fourteenth centuries, but these contain no detailed reports about the cultural practices of the inhabitants.[9] Moreover, archaeological evidence and the results of linguistic and paleographic studies are scanty and hence inconclusive.

The anthropologist H. Otley Beyer believed that the different peoples in the Philippine archipelago were the products of "wave migrations" from mainland Asia in prehistoric times.[10] Later historians and anthropologists, however, consider this theory with some skepticism as it could not offer a convincing account of the ethnolinguistic divergences among the Filipino cultural groups.[11] William Henry Scott, one of the few authorities on Philippine prehistory, favors a "filtering in" process of migration from mainland Asia.[12] His conclusions and arguments for a continuity between the Philippine Tabon cave man fifty thousand years ago and the present-day Filipino population enriched by the infusion of foreign blood through trade relations are much more compelling and convincing.

Under the present state of research along these lines, therefore, no categorical statement is possible as to the origin of the Filipinos, let alone the Ilocanos. However, if Scott's view of continuity and unity among Philippine groups before the arrival of the Spaniards is to be pursued, prehispanic and early Hispanic ethnohistorical documents describing the customs and beliefs of other ethnic groups, such as the Tagalogs and Visayans, may help shed light on the culture, the religious

[9] See William Henry Scott, *Prehispanic Source Materials for the Study of Philippine History*, rev. ed. (Quezon City: New Day Publishers, 1984) 135–40.

[10] H. Otley Beyer, "Outline Review of Philippine Archaeology by Islands and Provinces," *Philippine Journal of Science* LXXVII (July–August 1947) 205–390. See also his article, "Philippine and East Asian Archaeology and Its Relation to the Origins of the Pacific Islands Population," *National Research Council Bulletin* 29 (1948).

[11] F. Landa Jocano, for example, challenges Beyer's assumptions and conclusions in "Beyer's Theory on Filipino Prehistory and Culture: An Alternative Approach to the Problem," *Studies in Philippine Anthropology: In Honor of H. Otley Beyer*, ed. Mario Zamora (Quezon City: Alemar Publishers, 1967) 128–50.

[12] Scott, *Prehispanic Source Materials*, esp. 136–40.

beliefs, and practices of the pre-colonial Ilocanos. Most of these documents were either written by Spanish conquerors and bishops as official reports to the king of Spain or are chronicles written by missionary friars of the different religious orders. Given the religious, sociopolitical climate at that time and the cultural background of the authors, these accounts sometimes reveal the ethnocentric attitudes of the authors as well as the colonialist notion that subject peoples were congenitally inferior.[13] A critical reading of these materials, therefore, is important, carefully distinguishing between practices and the meanings ascribed to them.

PRE-CHRISTIAN MARRIAGE CUSTOMS

A more general word is first necessary about the religion of these peoples.

Pre-Colonial Religion: Anitism

The religious system which preceded Christian evangelization may be described as "anitism,"[14] a belief-system that hinges around the *anitos* or spirits. Knowing something about it provides a hermeneutical key to the appreciation of the Ilocano conviction that marriage is always a religious affair or has a religious dimension.

As early as 1586, the Spanish friar-chronicler Juan Gonzalez de Mendoza had written: "In certain adjacent islands, called the Ilocos, they worshiped the devil, offering him many sacrifices in payment and gratitude for the quantities of gold that he gave them."[15]

In 1640 the Jesuit Diego de Bobadilla writes that "all the religion of those Indians (the Filipino natives), is founded on tradition, and on a

[13] Phelan, *The Hispanization,* 38.

[14] Most anthropologists and historians refer to this phenomenon as animism, but anitism better expresses the reality. A more thorough description of this is found in Stephen K. Hislop, "Anitism: A Survey of Religious Beliefs Native to the Philippines," *Asian Studies* 9 (August 1971) 144–56. See also Edward Burnett Tylor, *Religion in Primitive Culture,* rev. ed. (New York: Harper Brothers Publishers, 1958) 9–11.

[15] Juan Gonzalez de Mendoza, "History of the Most Notable Things, the Rites and Customs of the Great Kingdom of China," *The Philippine Islands 1493–1898,* vol. VI, ed. Emma Helen Blair and James Alexander Robertson (Cleveland: Arthur H. Clark Company, 1905) 146. Henceforth this will be cited as Blair and Robertson. The English translations are the editors'. Abandoning military life for the Augustinian Order, de Mendoza was one of the three envoys sent to China by King Felipe II in 1576. Various obstacles, however, prevented them from going there until 1584. See also Antonio de Morga, "Sucesos de las Islas Filipinas" (Madrid: 1609), Blair and Robertson, vol. XVI, 131. This work of de Morga covers the events in the Philippine Islands from 1565 to 1603.

custom introduced by the devil himself, who formerly spoke to them by the mouth of their idols and of their priests."[16] The Augustinian friar Andres San Nicolas, in his "General History of the Discalced Augustinian Fathers," provides more information:

"The worship with which they reverenced their false deities they were wont to perform not in the villages, but outside them in the mountains, or the part nearest to their fields. They had certain little houses there like chapels, in which they all assembled. But that did not prevent them from having gods—penates, or idols, which they called *anitos*. The priesthood was exercised by certain old men, ceremonious in the extreme, and not less by old women called *catalonas*—witches, superstitious creatures, diviners, and casters of lots—who were esteemed and so thoroughly believed that whatever they said, although lies, was taken as an infallible oracle. The manner of their sacrifices (which they called by the name *maganitos*), on meeting to make them in the place that we have spoken of above, was none other than that, having prepared an unclean animal, very well grown—or for lack of it, a large cock—they offered it to the devil by means of one of those witches, with peculiar and curious ceremonies."[17]

From these accounts it becomes apparent that the devil-worship referred to by the Spaniards is identical with the early Filipino practice of anitism or the worship of nature spirits, deities or spirits of localities or activities, and of their own ancestors.[18] These ancestral spirits were venerated as personal guardians or companions. They receive not only formal worship conducted by priests and priestesses but also domestic offerings and routine acts of reverence.

Concerning the *anitos* of the early Ilocanos, Foronda adopts de los Reyes' classification.[19] This includes belief in those primitive spirits of persons who perished violently and may be buried beneath a tree and

[16] Diego de Bobadilla, "Relation of the Filipinas Islands," Blair and Robertson, vol. XXIX, 282.

[17] Fray Andres San Nicolas, "Historia general de los religiosos descalzos del orden de los ermitaños del gran padre y doctor de la iglesia san agustin de la congregación de españa y de las indias" (Madrid, 1664). English translation in Blair and Robertson, vol. XXI, 137.

[18] Scott makes the same claim about the Visayans at the time of the Spanish advent. See his article, "Visayan Religion at the Time of Spanish Advent," *Philippiniana Sacra* XXV (1990) 398.

[19] Isabelo de los Reyes, *Historia de Ilocos*, vol. I (Manila: Establecimiento Tipografico la Opinion, 1890) 155–74; quoted in Foronda, "The Establishment of the First

from whom the Ilocanos asked permission to penetrate a forest or to cut trees.[20] Then there are those who take visible forms as humans or as giants and possess a boat which travels like a balloon in the air, in search of dead human bodies. Besides these, there were minor spirits, those of the sea and the rivers, or the forests, or simply the spirits of the dead who continue to roam.

What this veneration reveals is the close affinity that the people had, and still have to this day, with nature and with dead ancestors. This should not be taken to mean that they were polytheistic. José Resurrección Calip argues that this was not the case.[21] He writes: "The Ilokos were not a polytheistic people, have never been one in fact. It is likely that the early or middle protohistoric period brought to them an exotic belief in the one supreme being, later augmented and finally substituted with one of a western seal."[22]

PRE-COLONIAL MARRIAGE CUSTOMS AND PRACTICES

Against this background we can consider marriage customs and beliefs. While documentary evidence is scant, we have some ethno-historical accounts that give bits and pieces of information that allow the reconstruction of pre-colonial Ilocano customs, practices, and beliefs surrounding marriage. Some information and insight may also be gained from the pastoral letters of bishops who served in the region as well as official documents such as the decrees of the synods held during the Spanish times.[23]

Missionary Centers in Ilocos (1572–1612)," *Ilocos Review* III (1971) 5. We shall refrain here from giving the names by which these spirits are called.

[20] Actually, it is still the common practice in the rural Ilocos to ask permission from these spirits, the *mangmangkik,* before cutting a tree or in passing a place believed to be inhabited by *anitos.*

[21] José Resurrección Calip, "The Iloko Epic, Lam-ang" (Ph.D. dissertation, University of Santo Tomas, 1957) 26–7; quoted in Foronda, "The Establishment," 5.

[22] Calip, "The Iloko Epic," 27.

[23] See Miguel de Loarca, "Relación de las Islas Filipinas," Blair and Robertson, vol. V, 34–187. Loarca came to the Philippines before the year 1576, traveled around the whole archipelago, and was later *encomendero* of the island of Panay. This included the duty of making provisions for the church and the local friar. See John Leddy Phelan, "Prebaptismal Instruction and the Administration of Baptism in the Philippines during the Sixteenth Century," *Studies in Philippine Church History,* ed. Gerald H. Anderson (Ithaca, N.Y./London: Cornell University Press, 1969) 29–31.

It has been maintained that early Filipinos were generally monogamous, although polygamy was practiced, to some extent.[24] More noteworthy is the fact that ethnohistorical documents seem to indicate that marriage customs and practices among the early Filipinos varied according to the family's place in the social strata. Loarca reports that in the sixteenth century "there appear to be three ranks of men in these islands—namely, chiefs, *timaguas*, who are freemen, and slaves—each class having different marriage customs."[25]

The most elaborate ceremonial accompanied marriage among the families of chiefs. The accounts available to us present at least three stages: the preparatory, the negotiation stage, and the marriage ceremony itself. Preparation involved the sending of envoys by the man to the house of the woman he wished to marry. The envoy, a young kinsman, planted a spear in the staircase of the house and invoked its gods and ancestors.[26] Negotiations that followed revolved mainly around the dowry, which among early Filipinos was given by the man's family to that of the woman.

There is evidence that in earlier times some Filipino parents made arrangements for the marriage of their children while they were still young.[27] The Ilocanos are said to have had a practice of betrothal, which they called *taní*.[28] This is an instance where parents of both parties, especially fathers, agree to have their daughter and son, who are still babies, marry each other as soon as they grow up. The parents of the boy were then expected to give presents to the girl's parents during the period between betrothal and marriage. This illustrates very clearly that marriage was considered a matter between families.

When the couple reach marriageable age, the parents of the boy and other relatives proceed to the house of the girl to remind her parents of the betrothal. It is at this time that the dowry was presented by

[24] See Pedro Chirino, "Relación de las Islas Filipinas," Blair and Robertson, vol. XII, 293.

[25] See Loarca, "Relación de las Islas Filipinas," 154–5. A critical study of early Filipino class structure is given in William Henry Scott, "Filipino Class Structure in the Sixteenth Century," *Cracks in the Parchment Curtain and Other Essays in Philippine History* (Quezon City: New Day Publishers, 1982) 96–126. See also Horacio de la Costa, *Readings in Philippine History* (Makati: Bookmark, 1965) 3–5.

[26] Loarca, "Relación de las Islas Filipinas," 155.

[27] Juan de Plasencia, "Customs of the Tagalogs," Blair and Robertson, vol. VII, 184.

[28] Alejandro Dumlao, "Ancient Marriage Customs Among the Ilocanos," *The College Folio* I (February 1911) 135.

the boy's family to the girl's parents. Added to this was payment for the milk which nourished the girl when she was still a baby.[29] If payment were impossible, the boy might be required to render personal service to the family of the girl in lieu of this.

The Marriage Ceremony

Loarca, in his relation, describes the marriage ceremony as follows:

"After the marriage is agreed upon—that is to say, after fixing the amount of the dowry which the husband pays to the wife . . . they go to bring the bride from the house of her parents. One of the Indians[30] takes her on his shoulders; and on arriving at the foot of the stairway to the bridegroom's house, she affects coyness, and says that she will not enter. When many entreaties have proved useless, the father-in-law comes out and promises to give her a slave if she will go up. She mounts the staircase, for the slave; but when she reaches the top of the stairway and looks into her father-in-law's house and sees the people assembled within, she again pretends to be bashful, and the father-in-law must give her another slave. After she has entered, the same thing takes place; and he must give her a jewel to make her sit down, another to make her begin to eat, and another before she will drink. While the betrothed pair are drinking together, an old man rises, and in a loud voice calls all to silence, as he wishes to speak. He says: 'So-and-so marries so-and-so, but on the condition that if the man should through dissolute conduct fail to support his wife, she will leave him, and shall not be obliged to return anything of the dowry that he has given her; and she shall have the freedom and permission to marry another man. Be all of you witnesses for me to this compact.' When the old man has ended his speech, they take a dish filled with clean, uncooked rice, an old woman comes and joins the hands of the pair, and lays them upon the rice. Then, holding their hands thus joined, she throws the rice over all those who are present at the banquet. Then the old woman gives a loud shout, and all answer her with a similar shout; and the marriage contract or ceremony is completed."[31]

[29] Ibid. The Tagalogs refer to it as *bigay-suso*, literally, "give-milk."

[30] As in Mexico, the word Indio or "Indian" was the term used by the Spaniards to refer to the native peoples in the Philippine Islands.

[31] See Loarca, "Relación de las Islas Filipinas," 154–7. For a somewhat different description see Francisco Colin, *Labor Evangelica* (1663), quoted in Serrano, "Towards a Cultural Adaptation of the Rite of Marriage," 134. Colin was a Jesuit priest who came to the Philippines in 1626 and worked as a missionary until his death in 1660.

In his *Cronicas* of 1738, the Franciscan missionary Juan Francisco San Antonio[32] noted that the natives also used what in Spain is called the "ex-of ring" *(sic)* to confirm the marriage contract and the consent of those contracting it. The bride and groom exchanged some jewelry while the family gave a sign of the acceptance of the dowry which had been promised. This was a sign similar to that which accompanied agreement over the sale of land, since of course the dowry often involved the exchange of land, produce, or things worked by hand such as jewelry or pottery.

There was no such elaborate negotiation or ceremonial among lower classes, because they owned no property. As Loarca explains, the principal ceremony of marriage was for the couple to drink together in the presence of guests, since this signified that the two were now one. Among slaves there was no ceremonial whatsoever but only the agreement to cohabit, though the master of the young man usually gave him a wedding gift.[33]

SOME OBSERVATIONS

The preceding survey on the marriage customs, practices, and beliefs of the Filipino natives at the first contact with the Spanish *conquistadores* and missionaries allows us to make the following observations and conclusions about their pre-Christian marriage practices. As the rite for chiefs show, marriage for the early Filipinos was considered a religious affair, in which the help of the gods and the *anitos* was invoked. This is also evident in the central role played by the local priests and priestesses who, in some cases, presided over the rite.

Marriage celebrations seem to have been primarily domestic. The rituals were, for the most part, performed either in the groom's or the bride's home. Noteworthy is the important part played by the elders of the community or clan, particularly in the marriage negotiations. This suggests the people's recognition that marriage is essentially a community affair. Moreover, there does not seem to be clear indications of discrimination due to gender differences.

The presentation of dowries and the rendering of personal service to the girl and her family does not only speak of the great esteem

[32] Fray Juan Francisco de San Antonio arrived in the Philippines sometime in 1724 and served in the Tagalog provinces until his death in 1774 in Manila.
[33] See Loarca, "Relación de las Islas Filipinas," 158–61.

given to women in Filipino society. It points as well to their acknowledgment of the seriousness of marriage itself. There is cognizance that marriage involves not only an individual's life and reputation, but also that it affects the existence of the tribe, the clan, the community. There is, likewise, a strong emphasis on the gift-character of the dowry, handed over in a gift-giving ceremony.

Not to be missed is the employment of native symbols in the marriage ceremony. The natives made use of available materials or objects, such as rice and lance, which carried a lot of significance for them, rice being their staple food and the lance their primary defensive or fighting instrument.

On the negative side, there is the discrimination among classes which affected marriage and its ceremonial. This was tied up with the socioeconomic conditions of the time. When in later times people broke out of this system and gained more independence and freedom, it is interesting that many of them incorporated elements of marriage negotiation and ritual among the families of chiefs. Some of these elements remain to this day. They show the continuing sense of kinship, the relation to land, the relation to the dead, and the prevailing persuasion that human relations are negotiated by an exchange of gift. These are obviously cultural factors to be taken into account in the Christian preparation and liturgy of marriage.

THE CONTRIBUTION OF THE SPANISH MISSIONARIES

In the process of evangelization the Spanish missionaries worked toward the eradication of customs and practices which they had perceived as contrary to the Christian religion. They wished to replace its rituals entirely with Christian worship.

It is important to recall once more that Spanish evangelization in the Philippines was a post-Tridentine reality. In order to guarantee orthodoxy and liturgical uniformity, the missionaries in Spanish Philippines followed the liturgical practices of Mexico, adopting for use in the islands the 1560 *Manuale Sacramentorum secundum usum ecclesiae Mexicanae*.[34] A reason for its adoption was the fact that the diocese of Manila,

[34] The complete title reads, *Manuale Sacramentorum secundum usum eclesiae Mexicanae. Noviter impressum, cum quibusdam additionibus utilissimis: que omnia in sequenti pagella reperies* (Mexico: 1560). A critical study of this manual can be found in Jakob Baumgartner, *Mission und Liturgie in Mexiko*. Vol. 2: *Die Ersten Liturgischen Bücher in der Neuen Welt* (Schoeneck/Beckenried: NZM, 1972) 147–77; for the liturgical texts see 316–28.

which then covered the whole archipelago, was a suffragan of Mexico, and it continued to be so even after it became an archdiocese in 1595.

To expedite the evangelical work of their members and to maintain liturgical uniformity, ritual books were prepared by the different religious congregations. In 1630, the Augustinian Ritual prepared by Fray Alonso de Mentrida was published. Its title, *Ritual para administrar los santos sacramentos, sacado casí todo del Ritual Romano, y lo demas del Ritual Indico,* indicated that this Ritual is in accord with the Roman Ritual, and that prior to its publication the Mexican *Manuale Sacramentorum* or the *Ritual Indico* had been in use.[35] Presumably, this Augustinian Ritual was the one used by all other missionaries in the islands until the different orders produced their own. After a few decades, in 1669, the Dominican Ritual *(Ritual para la recta administración de los santos sacramentos y demás funciones sagradas pertenecientes a los párrocos)* came off the press. This was followed by the Jesuit Ritual *(Ritual para administrar los santos sacramentos, sacado del Romano y de otros Indicos, para el uso de los Padres Ministros de las Doctrinas de la Compañia de Jesús de Philipinas)* in 1692. The Franciscans came up with their own in 1756, the *Ritual para la recta administración de los santos sacramentos, y demás funciones parochiales: arreglado a el Ritual Romano, Apéndice Toledano, y Decretos de la Sagrada Congregación de Ritos.*[36] From the titles alone, one can surmise that one of the primary concerns of these rituals was the *recta administración* of the sacraments and other liturgical functions. Since all follow the prescriptions of the Council of Trent and its aftermath, there is not in face much difference between these ritual books. With the help of these ritual books and accompanying manuals, the missionaries were able to preserve orthodoxy and homogeneous liturgical practice.

[35] Fray Alonso de Mentrida, *Ritual para administrar los santos sacramentos, sacado casi todo del Ritual Romano, y lo demás del Ritual Indico. Con algunas advertencias necessarias para la administración de los sanctos sacramentos. Con una declaración sumaria de lo que los Religiosos Mendicantes pueden en las Indias por Privilegios Apostólicos, los quales se traen a la letra. Recopilado por Fr. Alonso de Mentrida, de la Orden de S. Agustín, para servicio y uso de los Ministros de su Orden en estas Islas Philippinas* (Manila: Imprenta de la Compaña de Jesus, 1630). What is being used here, however, is the 1669 edition of the Ritual, made available to the author by the University of Texas (Austin) Library. It is important to note that the author of this Ritual is a member of the Augustinian order, the group of religious to whom pastoral ministry in the Ilocos was entrusted.

[36] See Luis Balquiedra, "The Liturgical Principles Used by the Missionaries and the Missionary Background to the Christianization of the Philippines," *Philippiniana Sacra* XXX (1995) 24–5.

At the same time, for marriage rites there is an influence in the rituals of the Hispanic rite that preceded Trent and its reform of liturgical books. This is because the missionaries, in both Mexico and the Philippines, were familiar with this ancient Visigothic liturgy. Language also played its part since of course in celebrating marriage some use of the native languages was necessary in order to ensure the consent of the couple and the validity of the marriage. The Nuptial Mass and Blessing, however, remained in Latin. Translation into the vernacular was limited to the parts that have to do with determining the readiness of the natives in receiving the sacraments validly and fruitfully. On the other hand, by bringing the sacraments to the natives in the festive atmosphere of the Spanish late medieval and baroque festival, they succeeded in making the sacraments more appealing to a people who love to feast and celebrate.

One of the positive effects of the imposition of the Christian rite of marriage was the attempt at eliminating inequality among the people. In contrast with the discriminatory pre-Christian practice, where only the chiefs enjoyed the benefit of a complete marriage celebration, Catholicism guaranteed every couple the right to a marriage ceremony.

A Catholic Rite with Spanish Flavor

The official liturgical form of celebrating marriage was a blend of both Roman and Spanish elements. The framework and the prayers contained in the Roman Ritual of 1614 were adopted, as well as the prayer texts from the *Missa Pro Sponsis* of the 1570 *Missale Romanum*. In addition to these, certain prayers and rites traceable to the *Ritual Indico* of the Mexican Church, which borrowed these elements from the Manual of Toledo (Spain), found their way into the rite.

The most important addition from the Hispanic Rite was the blessing and giving of the arrhae.[37] This is mentioned in Isidore of Seville and is found in the *Liber Ordinum*. Isidore and the *Liber* incorporate this symbol into the ceremony of marriage and make of it a pledge of the bridegroom's fidelity to his spouse. It would seem, however, that the giving of gold rings belonged in Visigothic Law to the service of betrothal, and was in the nature of the gift given by the bridegroom to the bride's family in demanding her hand in marriage. In this case, it had to do with

[37] See Korbinian Ritzer, *Le mariage dans les églises chrétiennes* (Paris: Éditions du Cerf, 1970) 300–2. The *arrhae* were a gift presented to the bride which often consisted of several gold rings, tokens of the wealth which the bridegroom bestowed on his bride. Historically, this ceremony preceded the later exchange of wedding rings.

the exchange of wealth between families, necessary to contracting marriage. In his ritual, de Mentrida adopts the rite according to the meaning of the *Manuale Sacramentorum* of Mexico, adopted from the *Liber Ordinum*. In the *Manuale,* when the man gives the arrhae to the bride, he says: "My spouse, I give you the arrhas as a sign of marriage: with my body I honor you, as it is commanded by the holy mother, the church of Rome."[38] This rite no longer refers to the property exchange of the original betrothal ceremony but has been given a spiritual significance.

In his treatment of marriage preparation, de Mentrida follows the prescriptions of the *Rituale Romanum,* with a few exceptions designed to meet the situation in the Philippines. Though it is customary in the Church to celebrate the marriage in the parish of the bride, the couple remain free to request that it be celebrated elsewhere. He notes that this is allowed to avoid litigation.[39]

With regard to the marriage rite, the ritual also allows for some accommodations. The marriage can be celebrated in any place and at any time, but the nuptial blessing is to be given only in the church. This prescription would allow for domestic rites of marriage, and for marriage in the home of one of the partners, and also allow for an ecclesiastical ceremony, with Mass and nuptial blessing to take place at a later date. This is remarkably similar to the ruling in the revised Roman ritual, number 44, that allows the marriage to be celebrated in the home, and makes room for marriage rites over a period of some days, while also noting the specific importance of the nuptial blessing.

Thus the celebration of the sacrament of marriage introduced by the missionaries was truly Roman but with a considerable Spanish flavor. Elements such as the two rings, arrhae, candles, and some prayers, which have been incorporated in the Mexican ritual, found their way into the Philippine ritual as well. Later on, other elements, particularly the use of veil and cord from the Manual of Toledo, would further enrich it.

MARRIAGE CUSTOMS AFTER THE ENCOUNTER WITH CHRISTIANITY

Even with the introduction of the Catholic ritual for the sacrament, the Filipino practice of celebrating marriage in different stages remained. While they submitted themselves to the canonical and legal

[38] See Baumgartner, *Mission und Liturgie in Mexiko,* 319.
[39] Ibid., 86, n. 5.

requirements of marriage, people also continued with their own domestic and religious rituals. The process of getting married in the Ilocos, during the Spanish regime, appears to have consisted of several stages: the marriage negotiations which had its climax in the betrothal or engagement in the home, the marriage ceremony in the church, the wedding banquet on the same day, and some other post-wedding ceremonies in the home.[40]

Marriage Negotiations and Betrothal

The general practice among the natives during the Spanish times seems to have been that when a man wanted to marry a woman, a party of elders and members of his family was assembled to negotiate with the woman's family. The marriage proposal was couched in words of native poems and songs sung to the accompaniment of a native stringed instrument. The negotiations, made in the presence of the prospective bride and groom, essentially revolved around the dowry which was to be presented to the woman and her family. This usually consisted of a parcel or parcels of land, but other payments were also promised to meet wedding expenses. When the marriage offer had been accepted, and all the details of the wedding discussed, a betrothal ceremony was held to signify that the two were engaged. It was usually held in the house of the groom.

Sometimes to make up for the insufficiency of the dowry, the young man lived in the house of the prospective bride to render service to the family. Bishops several times denounced this practice but it was hard to eradicate. Writing in 1768, Bishop Miguel Garcia of Nueva Segovia relates in his pastoral letter that a number of declarations and pronouncements had been issued condemning this custom.[41] Despite all protests, the practice continued even into the nineteenth century.

Marriage Ceremony

The marriage liturgy on the day of the wedding itself was done according to the ritual described above. Sometimes it seems the nuptial

[40] See Rodolfo Reyno, "Customary Wedding Among the Ilocanos," *Philippine Magazine* 35 (July 1938) 336, 346, 348; Alejandro Dumlao, "Ancient Marriage Customs Among the Ilocanos," *The College Folio* I (February 1911) 135–41.

[41] Bishop Miguel García, *Carta Pastoral, 1768*, Archivo de Santo Tomás, Libros t. 27, 156–7, quoted in Excelso García, "Particular Discipline on Marriage in the Philippines During the Spanish Regime," *Philippiniana Sacra* VIII (January–April

blessing was given only on the following day,[42] though Church authorities frowned on this as a rule.

When the ceremonies in church were over, everyone proceeded to the house of the bridegroom or some other place designated for the wedding banquet.[43] For the more affluent, the procession was often accompanied by a band of musicians. Upon their arrival at the house, the newlywed couple was met by a boy and a girl with lighted candles and led into the house altar where they knelt down while some prayers for them were recited. In some cases a song was also chanted. During the prayers they sat on each side of the altar. The wedding banquet ensued, where the bride and groom were made to feed one another. Dancing followed as soon as the couple finished their meal. Later in the afternoon, there was a ritual to mark the inclusion of the groom into the bride's family and clan, and the couple and their parents, relatives, and other guests then went to the bride's house. They were accompanied by a procession with music, song, and dance. Relatives of the groom carried symbolic goods, such as a mat, two pillows, a blanket, some foodstuff such as rice and eggs, some articles of his clothing, a yoke and a coil of rope, and other things that a new couple needed in order to learn to live independently. When they arrived at the house, relatives of the bride met them at the stairs and threw leaves and flowers upon the couple as they went up into the house, where they continued the merrymaking until sundown.

The marriage feast or celebration did not end on the wedding day but continued until the day of the *posíng*,[44] which means "weaning," "separation," or "taming." It refers to the fact that the couple now had to be separated from their families, be "weaned" from their parents, and begin to live on their own. This ceremony could be quite elaborate, full of admonitions from parents and relatives and symbolic gift-giving.

The missionaries reacted unfavorably to many of the natives' common customs, but despite this Filipino Catholics tended to incorporate their pre-Christian rituals into their celebrations of marriage.

1973) 20. From 1768 to 1779 Miguel García was bishop of Nueva Segovia, which then comprised the whole of Northern Luzon.

[42] Ma. Caridad Barrion, "Religious Life of the Laity in Eighteenth-Century Philippines as Reflected in the Decrees of the Council of Manila of 1771 and the Synod of Calasiao of 1773," *Boletin Ecclesiastico de Filipinas* XXIV (September 1960) 564.

[43] Dumlao, "Ancient Marriage Customs," 138–40.

[44] Ibid., 139–40.

Often enough, the line between true Christian worship and anitism was crossed. There is no denying that many of the Church's concerns were legitimate, but we also need to note the natives' attempt to make sense out of their newfound world, to reconcile their "pagan" customs and superstitions with their Christian beliefs. And with the passing of time, those pre-Christian rituals and beliefs which survived the conquest gradually lost their original religious identity and blended into popular religiosity or folk Catholicism. But it is not always easy to sort out what derives from pre-colonial times and what derives from Spanish Catholic practices.

Summary

This historical and ethnohistorical survey unfolds the complexity of the development of marriage ceremony in the Ilocos. A few things, however, stand out that are important to current liturgical inculturation.

The survey manifests that for the early Ilocanos entering marriage was a process which consisted of different stages. This strongly suggests the possibility of sequential rites, a *ritus continuus,* in the celebration of marriage itself. This would entail expanding on the ceremony done in church, so that the marriage itself and the nuptial blessing can be done in different places and on different days, thus accommodating indigenous customs.

There is, too, the symbolic value of the rites expressing family relations, including relation to ancestors and to the future of kin, as well as expressing the nature of the relation between man and woman in marriage. Although no serious attempts were made to translate and adapt the whole rite of marriage into the vernacular, the people used their indigenous languages for such rites as the exchange of consent, in the rites of giving gifts, and in the songs they sang during the wedding celebrations. This points to the necessity of creating marriage rituals that truly express the genius of the peoples' language and culture.

Likewise, some of the Ilocano traditional rites, such as the wedding feast, the singing and dancing, the sprinkling with rice grains, the giving of gifts, are symbolically rich. Not only do they express communal joy and support of the conjugal union and its success, they also signify the people's recognition of the vital importance of the marriage institution in the life of the community. The retrieval and incorporation of these rites seem to be an imperative in the preparation of new marriage rituals.

Marriage transactions, customs, and rites took place for the people of the Ilocos within a *religious* worldview, and in connection with an agrarian economy. At the heart of this were the *anitos,* belief in whom reflects a strong sense of the human person's connection with the world of spirits and of nature, so that they mediate between generations the relation between people and the land, and the changing relations between families when persons enter into marriage. Within this context, there was the sense of kin, of family, of couple, of human person, that is reflected in the customs studied in this chapter. This is always related to a worldview that makes sense of the way in which people live and supports certain kinds of procedures and relationships.

While it is to be admitted that excess and superstition were possibly involved in the natives' religious beliefs, festivities, and other practices surrounding marriage, this should not lead us to a total dismissal or denigration of some of the rites or of family festivities.

CONTEMPORARY CELEBRATION

Many of these customs survive in the Ilocos today, as well as the stress on kinship and attitudes to the land with which the people identify. Veneration of ancestors, especially the more recent dead, is also strong in the hearts of the people. Even when young people leave the region or migrate to other countries, the old way of getting married, with its mixture of kinship, domestic, and church rituals, often remains important to them. They will marry civilly elsewhere but wait for an opportunity to return to their native town or village before having a church wedding, since it can then be done along with observance of all the other customs, and with extended family in attendance.

On the other hand, while people still see entering marriage as a process, this process has lost some of its traditional ritual. The betrothal service has been largely replaced by the premarital investigation done by the priest. Families still negotiate marriage settlements but since this is done without benefit of ritual it has taken on a more secular value, losing its religious significance. Premarriage courses have replaced many of the ceremonies that belonged in homes and were celebrated among kin. The challenge of an inculturated liturgy is to restore some of the domestic and religious ceremonial to the process without falling prey to romanticism about the past.

Even with revisions introduced after the Second Vatican Council, the marriage ceremony itself still incorporates the giving of the arrhae. The Marriage Rite approved for the region in 1973 gives this

formula for the blessing: "Bless, O Lord, your servants with suffi-
ciency of material possessions which these arrhae symbolize so that
they may use them to attain eternal life. Through Christ our Lord." In
giving the arrhae to the bride, the groom says: "I give you these arrhae as a pledge of my dedication to your welfare. In the name of the
Father and of the Son and of the Holy Spirit." These formulas are not
those found in the Hispanic Rite or in the Manual of de Mentrida. In
fact, they retrieve something of the significance this exchange had
under ancient Visigothic law and custom, when the exchange of
wealth was done at the time of betrothal. Celebrated in the Philippine
Rite, it makes of the rite a pledge of the groom to the material welfare
of his bride and endows this with a sense of gift-giving.

Two ceremonies that have been added to the marriage service in
more recent times are the veiling of the couple and tying of the nuptial
cord. For the first, a designated pair lay the *velo*, a white veil, on the
shoulders of the groom and head of the bride. The use of veil in marriage is probably of Roman origin, wherein brides were covered completely by the *flammeum*, a red veil which served as a symbol of purity
and protection against evil spirits. The practice is mentioned in the
Liber Ordinum (1056), immediately after the order of the arrhae. The
girl's parents or other relatives hand her over to the priest, who veils
the couple with a pall or sheet, she completely and he over his shoulders only. Isidore of Seville associated this veiling to a priestly blessing.
Invoking the example of Rebecca, he saw this ceremony as symbolizing
the wife's subjection to the husband. It is a reminder for wives to practice womanly modesty before their husbands. Over the years, the veil
has taken on new symbolism. For some it is a sign of virginity. For others it is another sign of the marriage union. Still others interpret this as
symbolizing the roof of the new home the couple will build.[45]

The veiling is immediately followed by the placing of the cord (also
known as *yugal* or yoke), which is placed in the form of an eight over
the shoulders of the bride and bridegroom.[46] This is supposed to sym-

---

[45] See Mark Searle and Kenneth Stevenson, eds., *Documents of the Marriage Liturgy*
(Collegeville: The Liturgical Press, 1992) 118 and 125; Kenneth Stevenson, *Nuptial
Blessing: A Study of Christian Marriage Rites*, Alcuin Club Collections 64 (London:
SPCK, 1982) 62; Instituto de Liturgia Hispana, *Gift and Promise: Customs and Tradi-
tions in Hispanic Rites of Marriage* (Portland: Oregon Catholic Press, 1997) 7–8.

[46] Isidore of Seville sees in the cord a symbol of the marital bond or union. In his
time the cord was woven of white and purple color, the former standing for purity

bolize the matrimonial union and the couple's equal responsibility toward the marriage and the family they are going to build.

CONCLUSION: TOWARD AN ILOCANO RITE OF MARRIAGE

In the preparation of a marriage rite for the Ilocanos, one must take into account the abovementioned considerations. Given the pivotal role that religious rituals play in the lives of believers, it is important to develop rituals which effectively reflect the people's ethos and worldview so that the gospel and the liturgy may take root in their culture and in their lives. It is only when such rituals respect and pay attention to their "stories" and their visions of the world and reality that they become the powerful symbols they are meant to be, that is, linking the sacred and profane, the visible and invisible. For the marriage ritual to be "an instrument of salvation" for the participants, mediating what Geertz calls the "leap into the framework of the sacred," it must allow them to see how the transcendent is related to their own lives. They should be able to see their own lives, histories, their meaning-system mirrored in the rituals. For the Ilocos, what is needed then is an inculturated marriage ritual, a Christian marriage liturgy which the Ilocanos can identify as their own.

The work of preparing this kind of ritual, however, is not without difficulties. It must contend with certain issues which when ignored would render the ritual less effective, perfunctory, or perhaps even alienating and bereft of meaning. In brief, a new marriage ritual in Ilocano must likewise address present-day realities.

One of these realities is the constant evolution that the Ilocano culture, indeed every culture, is undergoing. Caught in the web of rapid transition from rural to more urbanized context, from a predominantly agricultural to industrial setting, the people's way of life, for better or worse, is experiencing certain modifications. Correspondingly, these cultural shifts, especially their relation to land, are causing partial dissolution of their religious worldview. Concomitant with the people's gradual loss of attachment and appreciation of traditional values, customs, and rituals is the incremental disintegration of their ancient and distinctive ethos and meaning-system. The intent of an inculturated ritual is not to preserve traditional cultural elements whose significance is no longer evident and hence whose power to

---

of life, the latter for the blood of [bearing] children. See Searle and Stevenson, *Documents of the Marriage Liturgy,* 118–9.

influence people's lives is already in serious question. It seeks rather to dialogue with the people's culture which, while constantly evolving, also embodies firmly established values and traditions which have shaped their lives and institutions through the years.

Related to cultural transitions is the growing independence on the part of young people in choosing their marriage partners, even though they retain a strong sense of family and kin. More than ever, the younger population in the region is getting more mobile in pursuit of education or in search of jobs. With the expansion of their world is the widening of opportunities to meet and, in many cases, intermarry with peoples of other cultures, socioeconomic, and religious backgrounds. And because of these differences, many of the Ilocano customs, traditions, and beliefs about marriage run the risk of being unappreciated or misunderstood. The preparation of an Ilocano marriage ritual has to consider this reality, too. While acknowledging and affirming the freedom of the parties in their choice of partners, it also has to discover ways to reinforce the sense of family and kin which is a fundamental component in the Ilocano's individual and communal existence.

Accessory to rapid urbanization and industrialization is the gradual secularization of marriage. Under the guise of being pragmatic, a growing number of young people today are deliberately choosing to exchange vows before a civil authority while postponing the celebration of their marriage in church or skipping it altogether. Meanwhile, there is the growing phenomenon of couples living together with the benefit of neither a civil nor a religious ceremony. And many of those who celebrate their marriage in church have the propensity to add certain rituals practiced in foreign countries like the United States without a clear knowledge of their significance.[47] But because of a strong "colonial mentality" they do them anyway because they originate from a foreign country.[48] These are realities that have to be taken into consideration as well. How would a new marriage ritual respond to these phenomena?

Despite the rapid cultural transitions that affect the lives of the people in the Ilocos at present, there remain some firmly established

[47] There is some recent Western influence, as in the throwing of the bride's garter to the bachelors present.
[48] "Colonial mentality" is that kind of thinking which considers anything local as always inferior to that which comes from a colonizing country.

values and stable cultural elements that are not so clearly integrated into their religious framework. If the objective of liturgical inculturation is the integration of worship and culture, then these values and cultural elements are precisely those that need to be addressed in the creation of rituals. A fine example is the strong sense of family and kinship and relatedness to land and nature, which pervades the whole meaning-system of the Ilocanos. In spite of Vatican II's emphasis on the importance of signs and symbols and the communal character of every liturgical celebration, the revised rituals do not seem to go far enough to give the consideration these values deserve. It would seem that if one were to respect these values, serious consideration would likewise have to be given to the domestic rituals that the Ilocanos celebrate on the occasion of marriage and the various signs and symbols they use. Consequently, this would imply the adoption of a new ritual framework integrating the various cultural elements within a revised order or sequence of rites accompanied by formulas that explain the meaning of these rites while genuinely expressing the genius of the people's language, their worldview and ethos, indeed, their "webs of significance."

Chapter VI

Toward a Contextualized Ilocano Rite of Marriage

In this chapter, the objective is to present the particular shape and form of a contextualized Ilocano marriage rite, its ritual framework, and its components. The author has composed a complete rite in the Ilocano language. What is presented here is an outline with some indications of how the rite attends to context, language, and symbol.

While the overall method followed is that of contextualization as described in Chapter III, other procedures noted by Chupungco are incorporated. In the translation of suitable prayer texts found in the Roman Ritual the principles of dynamic equivalence can be used. At the same time, in the composition of new texts creative assimilation is helpful in incorporating traditional rites and prayers in Ilocano, drawing on the language and on texts traditional to the local culture. The same may be said concerning symbols, symbolic gestures, and music.

A NEW RITUAL FRAMEWORK: A CONTINUOUS RITE

When we take the Ilocano culture as a starting point in preparing a marriage rite, the extended celebration of Ilocano marriages points toward what the Roman liturgy calls a *ritus continuus*, that is, a continuous set of rituals spread out over a period of time to respond to the stages of a process. This begins with betrothal or engagement and integrates what is done in church with what is done in the home before and after the wedding rites. An extended ritual such as this gives the attention and respect to elements in the culture that are positive. It is useful in helping the people discover their true identity and promotes their well-being. It is likewise a response to the increasing secularization of marriage celebrations resulting in the gradual neglect or downplaying of the sacred dimension.

It is quite remarkable that the Roman Rite now provides an order for the blessing of an engaged couple, a first time in the history of the Roman Rite. It is, however, placed in an appendix to the marriage ritual and needs to be integrated into a process of preparation for the wedding. In a contextualized rite of marriage for the Ilocos what is envisaged is one that fittingly commences with the celebration of engagement in the traditional family setting, reaches its highpoint at the liturgy in church, and concludes at the place of reception. The framework of such a rite may thus be described as a journey comprising four major stages: (1) celebration before the wedding, which is marked by the rite of engagement, preferably in the home; (2) a period of preparation for the wedding with the necessary catechesis which is marked by various rituals; (3) celebration on the day of the wedding, which includes the ceremonies in church and at the place of reception; and (4) celebration after the wedding, in the home.

RITE OF BETROTHAL OR ENGAGEMENT

In a continuous or extended celebration of marriage the rite of betrothal or engagement makes up the first stage of such a multi-phased process. It is a ritual celebration that fits perfectly within the Ilocano structure of marriage preparation. With regard to the shape and elements of this rite, it seems suitable and expedient to work with the order found in the Roman Ritual as a basis.

The rite is suitably celebrated in the house of the bride's parents, where marriage negotiations are settled. Since the celebration of engagement is by nature a domestic ritual, it is only appropriate that one of the parents should preside. The office of presiding at this ritual, however, may be delegated to a lay minister who belongs to the community or is related to either of the parties. To encourage greater participation, different roles in the rite, such as proclaiming the word or leading the intercessions, may be distributed among family members, with special attention to the part played by the parents. At the Liturgy of the Word, instead of a homily one of the parents or another respected layperson in the community may be allowed to give a piece of advice particularly to the couple. This fits with the nature of the traditional domestic celebration of engagement.

A number of traditional Ilocano customs could be placed before the blessing over the couple. This includes the signing of the document whereby the two pledge themselves to each other, an exchange of rings and gifts, the handing of the dowry to the woman, as well as the customary "bride compensation" to the mother.

In translating the prayer texts and formulas taken from the Roman Ritual, the principle of dynamic equivalence needs to be put to service, so as to respect the genius of the Ilocano language. In addition to these prayers, there needs to be a newly composed blessing of the dowry and other gifts before they are exchanged. What follows is an English translation of such a blessing written by the author in Ilocano:

"N. (bride-to-be), accept the gifts from the family of N. (bridegroom-to-be). May they serve to symbolize their heartfelt acceptance of you into their midst and their sincere concern for the welfare of the family you are going to build. May the Lord guide you so that you may treasure these gifts just as you cherish your love for each other."

What is highlighted in this text is the power of the gifts to cement the relationships between two families or clans. That is reinforced by the recommendation that instead of the prospective groom one of his parents or other representative of his family takes the role of presenting the gifts. The gifts are not the man's alone, but come from his family. As to what the gifts symbolize, two things are mentioned. First, they express the family's warm, heartfelt acceptance of the woman, an enthusiastic gesture of welcome to her as a new member of the family. They mark the bonding of two families in extended kinship. Second, gift-giving signifies their sincere concern for the future life of the man and woman as a couple, looking forward to establishing a family of their own. The formula takes into consideration the fact that what is usually given is either a piece of land, which the couple could use for agriculture or as a space on which their own house is built, or a certain amount of money which they could use to buy property or to start a business. The blessing thus takes into account the social and economic aspects of the relationship.

In the Ilocos, we need to remember the significance of the exchange of a piece of land. It has an extraordinary value that goes beyond the economic since it represents the recipients' connectedness with a living tradition. It is a powerful reminder of their being part of a network of relationships that include both the living and the dead. Here we simply have to remember that such a piece of land or property has been passed on from one generation to the next. It is precisely because of this quasi-sacred character of the gifts that the ceremony in which it is handed over ought to have a solemn and reverent character.

The author has also provided a formula for the handing over the "bride compensation" to the mother. The text is proposed for use in places where this custom is still observed. To avoid any insinuation that this gift is some kind of payment or even a "soft bribe" to the mother, people might want to consider presenting other forms of tokens, such as a rosary, a Bible, or something religious in nature. Moreover, there is good reason to suggest that the prospective bridegroom be the one to present the gift to his future mother-in-law as an expression of his gratitude and appreciation for the love and care she had showered on his future wife. The English translation of the blessing composed in Ilocano is as follows:

"This gift is offered to the mother of N. (future bride), who breast-fed her, carried her in her arms and cared for her needs. She loved and doted on her child from conception, who is soon going to leave her so that she and her future husband may establish their own household. May this token serve to signify appreciation for her many toils and sacrifices for the sake of her daughter."

The inclusion of this ritual in a celebration of engagement accentuates the Ilocano's great respect and esteem for parents and elders. While it affirms the primary role of the two parties in marriage, it likewise acknowledges the important place that their families and relatives occupy in their network of relationships. The ordinary Ilocano couple is conscious that the quality of their relationships with their families can and does make all the difference in their married life.

PREPARATION BEFORE THE MARRIAGE

The intervening period between the engagement and the wedding is envisaged as a period of intense spiritual preparation for the engaged couple. The nature of marriage as a lifelong covenantal relationship demands that those who enter into it prepare themselves adequately for the many challenges and difficulties this vocation presents.

This preparatory stage requires that catechesis be given to the engaged couples in order that they can celebrate the sacrament conscious of all that it entails. The different dioceses surely have their own so-called "pre-Cana" programs designed precisely to prepare couples for the reception of the sacrament of matrimony. The content, length, and other mechanics of the program, however, vary from one local church to another. One thing which seems to be common among them is the fact that such programs have a tendency to be too academic and cerebral. Activities appear to be limited only to lectures or sharing of experiences. Pre-Cana programs are abundant in intellectual exercises but short on rituals. This is an area that needs to be explored and taken advantage of. As a model we need only to consider the power and effectiveness of the rituals that embody the catechumenate, marking its various stages.

Catechesis and Ritual

What is being suggested here then is that before the scheduled wedding date engaged couples are to undergo a series of catechetical lessons on marriage, family life, and their role in the church community. Each session is to be carefully designed and formulated so that rituals and other activities which could help intensify and enhance their preparation are integrated.

The author has provided an outline and text for such celebrations in Ilocano. To give an example, during one of the sessions where the focus is on marriage as discipleship, a short ritual celebration is suggested to culminate the day's meeting. This service would include some Scripture readings, some reflections to help interiorize that which was discussed, appropriate prayers and songs, and some rites, such as sprinkling with holy water or presentation with a cross, which remind them of their baptismal commitment. For the giving of the cross, this formula, here translated from Ilocano, is suggested:

"My dear friends, the Lord Jesus said, 'Anyone who wishes to become my disciple must deny his/her [Ilocano has the same word for both] very self, take up his/her cross daily and follow in my footsteps.' We hand over to you this symbol of the cross that will serve as a reminder that you must always accept graciously the duties/responsibilities of the married state and build a home that will always live in obedience to Christ's will."

In similar fashion, a session centering on the role of the family in society could fittingly culminate with a prayer service that includes a handing-over of the Bible to the engaged couple to signify their duty later on as a Christian couple to live according to God's Word and help evangelize the world. On the issue of catechetical method, it is traditional in the Ilocos to instruct engaged couples through what is called the *albasya*, and elements of this might be incorporated into the service.

The *albasya* is sometimes part of the preliminary negotiations for marriage when the man's family visits the home of the woman. Two speakers, representing each of the parties to marriage negotiations, address the couple with a series of poems and questions. The text is long but the example is given here of the initial address and response in a text given to the author by an elder in a village of the Ilocos.

Entering the house, the speaker for the man's party says, "Hail Mary, most pure," and those inside respond, "Conceived without sin." The speaker then continues:

"Most adored place and spot where this barrio stands, a place of in-comparable cleanliness and beauty where this admired home of such joy is set, and to you the most honored and loving residents, the rela-tives who have come here on this blessed day and hour, may your gentle hearts hearken to our greetings as the Angel Gabriel, the great ambassador of God, greeted the Holy Virgin Mary at the oratory as she was made the Queen Empress crowned with glory. . . . The house is an empire, a place of repose . . . since Venus and the Moon light up the bright firmament, and they are my refuge as I call for the help of the three persons, God the Father, God the Son, and the Holy Spirit. I call on them to bring you all a pleasant afternoon."

To this greeting, the speaker for the woman's party responds:

"Thank you very much. We offer you our unspeakable appreciation for we have heard the names of the Three Persons. But we have been taken by fear and trembling as I behold you who have come from afar to surprise us. And this is what I can say to you, honorable head, that you allow us to inquire which place or town or kingdom you are com-ing from, because we are afraid that you are heretics who opposed the will of God or that you are enemies who have come to do us violence."

The first speaker responds at length, claiming inheritance from the children of Israel, led by Moses to the Promised Land, as well as from Melchisedech who blessed Abraham, and the Magi who came to visit the child Jesus and his mother at his birth. Finally he says:

"We have come to this noble place of yours without any other inten-tion than to look for the valued gift of the blessed sacrament of matri-mony through which our Lord Jesus Christ blesses us; for it cannot be constituted by one alone but must be a partnership, and they say that it is in this place that we can be assisted and succored in this desire for matrimony, hoping that you will not look down in disdain at the helplessness you behold and our evident life of poverty and frailty, my brothers/sisters."

The continued dialogue of salutation, question, and response includes much instruction in biblical history on the teachings of the Church about Christ and about the sacraments.

The style of this dialogue is itself an instruction in courtesy as well as in the complex nature of human relations. It suggests what it is to live always in God's presence and to identify one's own self and one's family by finding identity and one's own story in the divine plan of history. It depicts what it is for a young woman and man to leave family and earlier life behind in order to enter this relationship of marriage, which is itself full of mystery. It shows that marriage itself has to be seen within God's plan and against the landscape of the wonder of God's grace and gifts, given in God's Son. It fits the religious sense of the people that gives great honor in this story to the Virgin Mary. It is because of all this that it may model a catechesis that is readily integrated into a service of prayer, song, and ritual. Of course it would have to be adapted from its original spot as part of a visit of one family to another, but the core and style of what is proclaimed with praise and wonder could be kept.

Rite of Leave-Taking

Another possibility that can be considered is some form of a rite of leave-taking in which each family of the bride and the bridegroom gathers around its member who is soon going to leave the family to be united with his or her spouse. The Catholic Household Blessings and Prayers for the United States of America[1] provides a ritual model for the "Blessing of a Son or Daughter Before Marriage." This could be adapted with the necessary modifications so as to give it an Ilocano flavor and character.

Sometime during the engagement period, on a day close to the wedding date, the family and close relatives of the couple may gather together at the family home with a special meal. Before they sit down at table, however, they express their sentiments concerning the imminent departure or separation of one of their members through prayers, gesture, and song. One of the parents or an elder may be asked to lead this short service. After the sign of the cross and a brief greeting, an appropriate Scripture passage is proclaimed. A short

[1] Bishops' Committee on the Liturgy, *Catholic Household Blessings and Prayers* (Washington, D.C.: United States Catholic Conference, 1988) 240–2.

exhortation by either of the parents or another relative may be given at this time. This is to be followed by the presentation of a Bible, a cross, an image of the Lord or the Blessed Mother, or the family's patron saint. Intercessory prayers are then offered on behalf of the engaged couple, to be concluded with the Lord's Prayer. The prayer service fittingly ends with a final blessing of the future bride or bridegroom in which all in the assembly extend their hands or place their hands on him/her. After making the sign of the cross marking the culmination of the blessing service a suitable song may be sung.

The period of preparation before the wedding reaches a crescendo on the night before the wedding, at the dance party held at the house of either the bride or bridegroom. Aside from helping to intensify the festive atmosphere, the celebration is an occasion to welcome guests and to introduce relatives of both parties to one another. In the meantime, family members, relatives, and neighbors offer their services, in the spirit of love, neighborly cooperation, and aid, in the preparation of the place of reception and the food for the banquet, and in decorating the church.

CELEBRATIONS ON THE DAY OF THE WEDDING

The ritual we propose for the wedding day has three components: the simple rite of parental blessing in the home before the bride or the bridegroom leaves for the church, the wedding ceremonies in church, and the ceremonies at the place of reception.

A Simple Rite in the Home

To create and foster the proper disposition for the celebration of the sacrament, a simple rite in each home before the two parties leave for the church might help. Parents, through a short prayer and a simple gesture, can give their blessing to their son or daughter before he or she leaves the family home for the church for the wedding liturgy. Invoking the method of creative assimilation, this short but touching rite retrieves and brings to the fore a Filipino tradition in which children do the *máno* (kissing of the parents' hands) as a gesture of respect, reverence, and love whenever they leave home for travel or when they expect to be away for some time. Parents, in turn, bless their children by tracing the sign of the cross on their foreheads or simply make the sign of the cross over them with the simple invocation *"Dios ti manga-asi"* ("May God show mercy/kindness [on you]") or *"Dios ti mangaluad kenka"* ("May God be your protector/guide").[2] Here is an example of a social ritual that has been thoroughly Christianized, a cultural practice expressing Gospel values that has become a component of the people's religiosity.

The ritual proposed here is really short and simple. When everyone is ready to leave the house, the entourage of each party gathers together at a suitable place in the house for the parental blessing. Before each of the parents traces the sign of the cross on the forehead of their son or daughter, however, the following prayer may be said in Ilocano:

"Heavenly Father, we acknowledge that you are the source of all life and goodness. With your gift of children you give joy to the union of couples and it is You who determine each person's vocation in life. Look down upon N. your son/daughter, who is about to receive the sacrament of matrimony. Enlighten his/her heart and mind and strengthen his/her will so that each decision and action that he/she makes be always in accord with your will. May you allow this event to bring forth the fruits of deeper relationships among us and our families, thereby united in supporting our children and brother/sister who are getting married. We ask this through Christ your Son, our Lord."

This prayer highlights the important role of the families of both parties in guaranteeing that the success of this marriage is not left to chance. While it is acknowledged that this is ultimately in God's hands, it is also recognized that the families are responsible for giving all the needed support, whatever form this will take, for members who get married. Families of both parties then are challenged to unite, to come together and rally behind the couple. That is why a part of the prayer petitions that this event may bring about closer or deeper relationships among members of the families concerned. The Ilocano term for "bring forth fruit" is used to reflect the agricultural vocabulary of the people.

God is here acknowledged as Creator. The prayer confesses that children, who are sources of joy in marriage, are God's gifts to their families. That explains the reference to the fiancé or fiancée as God's child *(anakmo)*. Nothing is closer to the firm Ilocano conviction on children than this statement. This is probably one of the reasons why the typical Ilocano family is large. Christ is also invoked as *anak* ("child") of God.

---

[2] "Kissing the hand" is not to be taken literally here. The gesture actually consists in touching the other person's right hand with one's forehead. Aside from parents and elders (grandparents, uncles, aunts, godparents) it is also extended to priests.

When the prayer has been said, the parents trace the sign of the cross on the forehead of the groom or bride, accompanied by the following formula: "May the Lord Our God protect and guide you so that you may live in accordance with the calling he has intended for you." The formula preserves the biblical image of God familiar to Ilocanos as the protector and guide of his own people. It expresses the conviction that it is only with God's help that the person is able to live out faithfully the vocation or kind of life that is meant for him/her.

After the signing of the forehead with the sign of the cross, the man or woman may kiss his/her parents' hands. This popular Filipino practice parallels somewhat the gesture done during baptism where the candidate's forehead is signed with the cross by the parents and godparents, albeit with a different meaning, that is, to signify the child's being welcomed by the Christian community.

RITUAL CELEBRATION IN THE CHURCH

The liturgy that is being proposed here maintains the structure of the Roman Order for the Celebration of Marriage (1991), but inclusive of elements built around Ilocano cultural, religious, and social realities. It derives much inspiration from the Marriage Rite for the Philippines (1970) and its Ilocano translation, and the Tagalog Rite of Marriage (1983).[3] The 1970 rites basically follow the typical edition of the Roman Rite (1969), but with additional elements borrowed from the Toledan Ritual, such as the *arrhae*, the veil, and the cord, and the lighting of two candles. As already noted, much care has to be taken with translations from Latin texts, with the incorporation of ritual gestures and symbols, and in formulating the right formulas for such matters as the exchange of consent between the couple. While the author has reworked the entire ritual, since this publication is addressed to a wider readership, in what follows we limit ourselves to describing some of the more significant elements of Ilocano custom and ritual incorporated into the marriage rite.

---

[3] The rite is locally known as *Ang Pagdiriwang ng Pag-iisang Dibdib. Salin sa Tagalog ng Huwarang Sipi* (Manila: Panayam ng mga Katolikong Obispo ng Pilipinas, Lupon para sa Wikang Tagalog sa Liturhiya, 1983). It was prepared by Fr. Anscar Chupungco and his collaborators, approved by the Conference of Catholic Bishops, and was confirmed by the Sacred Congregation for the Sacraments and Divine Worship on April 20, 1983. Henceforth, it shall be quoted as 1983 Tagalog Rite.

Reception of the Couple

As soon as the presider, other ministers, the couple, and their entourage are ready, the procession to the altar or sanctuary begins. The liturgical ministers go first, followed by the priest. After them come the little girls who strew flower petals along the processional aisle, the couple's attendants (groomsmen and bridesmaids), the sponsors, and, finally, the bride and bridegroom accompanied by their parents.[4] Reaching the sanctuary the ministers make a gesture of reverence to the altar and the Blessed Sacrament (if the tabernacle is there) while the priest goes to the altar, reverences it with a bow, venerates it with a kiss, and then goes to his chair.[5] At the sanctuary, the couple make the *máno* (kissing the hands) to the parents of both before they occupy their designated seats close to the altar.

There seems to be a valid reason for dissuading couples from making the procession into a bride's grand and dramatic entrance. In the Ilocos, parents have already given their children to each other in the ceremonies that precede the wedding. The rubric in the 1970 Marriage Rite for the Philippines explicitly decrees that during the procession "all appearance of theatrical show must be avoided."[6]

In the desire to make the rite more expressive of the people's culture, the Tagalog Rite of Marriage has accommodated two cultural traditions during the procession: the strewing of flower petals along the processional aisle and the *máno* or kissing of the parents' hands by the couple. These two rituals are also popularly observed in the Ilocos and are here proposed as elements of the procession in the Ilocano Marriage Rite. These gestures serve not only to increase the festive atmosphere of the wedding, they likewise underline the role of the family or clan in marriage, as well as indicate the nature of the marital relationship within this culture. The *máno* is a Filipino cultural gesture of expressing the biblical injunction, "A man shall leave his father and mother and shall cling to his wife and the two shall become one" (Gen 2:24; Matt 19:5; Mark 10:7; Eph 5:31).

Nuptial Blessing

As already noted, due to Hispanic influence the rite for the Philippines includes the *arrhae*, the veil, and the cord. These are kept in this

---

[4] The Roman Order, no. 46, suggests a more simple procession.

[5] Order for the Celebration of Marriage, no. 47.

[6] CBCP, Marriage Rite for the Philippines, 10.

ritual, along with the elements of the Roman Rite. What is here offered is an original text for the Ilocano Nuptial Blessing, given in rough English translation.

This is an attempt to create a new text for the Nuptial Blessing that reflects the life of the Ilocano people who live off the land, takes the images of blessing that resonate with their lives, expresses their family and cultural values, while at the same time reflects the nature of marriage as covenant and sacrament. Its structure follows that of the traditional Christian blessing which consists of remembrance, thanksgiving, and epicletic intercession. The text recalls the works of creation and the mystery of Christ, and puts the blessing of marriage within this setting. In the invocation of the Holy Spirit, it makes intercession for blessings on the couple and on their families.

"Most loving Father, we praise and thank you for all the blessings which you have given us and especially for the blessings of marriage. In creating the world you caused life to abound in the waters and on the land. You richly endowed the earth with vegetation, plants and trees of every kind, and created living creatures that walk across its face. You filled the skies with many-colored birds and the waters with fish and mammals of many sorts.

"And so we say: R. *Glory to God who is so loving.*

"In the midst of these earthly wonders, you placed man and woman, making them according to your image and likeness, bidding them to live together in the bonds of love, and in peace with the earth and with all creatures that dwell on it. You commanded them to increase and multiply, so that through the blessings given to them and their families the praise and the glory of your name might resound down through the ages. And so we say: R. *Glory to God who is so loving.*

"In times of trouble and strife, the bond of marriage covenant continued to be a sign and an assurance of your covenant with creation and with a chosen people. When your own beloved Child, Jesus the Christ, came into the world to restore the peace and harmony disturbed by sin, he blessed this marriage bond, and filled couples with the grace that makes of them a living sign of the covenant and communion between Christ and his Church, united together as one body. And so we say: R. *Glory to God who is so loving.*

"In remembrance of Christ's presence at the marriage feast of Cana, and of the cleansing and life-giving waters that flowed upon his Church from his side on the Cross, we ask you Father, to send your Spirit upon this couple. May the power of this Spirit inflame their hearts, enlighten their minds, and strengthen their wills, so that they may live as your children in Christ, looking to you as the source and guarantee of every blessing.

"R. *Lord, may you send your Spirit upon them.*

"May they cling to one another in pure love and fidelity.

"May they enjoy the fruit of the land in peace and tranquility.

"May they be bearers of life and enrich their kin and your Church with the children whom they welcome into their lives as gifts from you. In every trial and sorrow, may they have your support, and in every joy may they rejoice in you.

"May their house and home be a hearth where others find hospitality and welcome, and where the poor and suffering find solace and comfort.

"May their parents and families too rejoice in this union and in the enrichment of their lives by these bonds of communion.

"May this couple, Father, be a blessing to their families, to the Church, and to the world.

"May they be witnesses of the covenant which you made with creation and which you have given to the Church in Christ, sealing it with the grace of the Spirit.

"May they with their families and friends be the sign to all of your grace and love, and after their journey in this life may they enter into the eternal home that you have promised to your children.

"Through Christ your Son, Our Lord.

"AMEN."

Some comment on Ilocano vocabulary will be helpful. The blessing prayer begins by addressing God as a loving Father (*nadungngo nga Ama*), an image that is familiar to Ilocanos, *nadungngo* being a word that is used to express intense, deep, and great love. God is looked upon as the source (*gubbuayan*) and guarantee (*talged*) of every blessing. Christ is referred to as *Anak* (child) of God, a name to which the people could relate well since among Ilocanos family relationships are of great value and within the family it is the children who are at the center, the focus of everyone's attention.

Using images evocative of the creation story in the book of Genesis, the formula blesses God for the gifts in creation—on land, in the sky, or in the waters. The people, with their agricultural and rural background, could certainly identify with such vocabulary. It is also within this creation story that human dignity is affirmed and that the beginnings of the vocation of marriage can be traced.

Throughout the prayer, the themes of marriage as a covenant *(tulag, katulagan)* and as sacrament *(senial, pagilasinan, sakramento)* loom large. It sees the marriage covenant between the man and the woman as a sign and assurance of God's covenant with creation and God's chosen people, as a living sign of the covenant between Christ and his Church. The close connection between marriage and baptism is also highlighted in mentioning the water that flowed from Christ's side on the cross and his presence and miracle at the wedding feast of Cana. At the epiclesis, what is asked on behalf of the couple is the blessing of their total being, their whole selves, their *panunot* (intellect), *puso* (heart), and *nakem* (will). This will enable them to live as God's children.

The petitions that are made on the couple's behalf repeat most of the intentions that we have seen in the various euchological texts, especially in the General Intercessions and solemn blessings. They are, however, articulated in a language that is reflective of the Ilocano environment and worldview. These include the blessings of mutual love and fidelity, offspring that will enrich the kin and the Church, fruitfulness of their labors, support in time of trial, hospitality extended to others especially the poor and needy, harmonious relationship with families and friends, witnessing before the community and the world, and eternal beatitude.

For more active participation among the people in the assembly we have introduced acclamations interspersed into the blessing prayer. An acclamation of praise is suggested as a congregational response after the recall of creation and the work of Christ. Another acclamation echoes the petition for the sending of the Holy Spirit upon the couple. At the end of the nuptial blessing the congregation is to respond with the Amen, which may be said or chanted. Should the presider find the text of the nuptial blessing rather lengthy he has the option to shorten it by omitting some of the petitions.

Celebration at the Place of Reception

After the ceremony in church, the couple and their guests proceed to the wedding reception. Whatever Ilocano rituals contribute to a cultural and Christian perception of marriage are to be retained.

RICE AND FLOWERS

One of the rituals referred to above is the showering of the couple with grains of rice and flower petals as they approach the house where the reception is to take place. Rice is of particular significance for the Ilocano people. Being their staple food, it is identical with life itself, with existence, with work, and with survival. It is indeed sometimes referred to as *grasya* or blessing. In showering the couple with grains of rice, their relatives and friends wish them the blessings of life itself.

To bring out the full human and religious significance of this action, a blessing could be pronounced over the rice and the flower petals as the couple are close to the house and before the grains and petals are thrown. Here is an English translation of the text proposed:

"N. and N., may the blessings that you receive from the Lord and the good works that you do to your fellow men and women be as abundant as the rice grains that come down upon you like rain from heaven. May your married life resemble the scent and fragrance of the flowers from paradise that adorn your path."

The formula uses images and metaphors that are familiar to the Ilocano people such as *tudo nga aggapu't langit* ("rain coming down from heaven"), *ayamuom ken banglo dagitoy sabasabong ti paraiso* ("the scent and fragrance of these flowers from paradise"). Coming from an agricultural background, the Ilocanos recognize the crucial importance of rain. Most of the agricultural land in the Ilocos is arid and rain-fed. Little rain or the absence of it brings crisis and no produce. For the Ilocano, rain comes down as heaven's blessing. What is asked from God is abundant *(nabuslon)* blessings. In turn, what is asked of the couple is abundant good works *(naimbag nga aramid)* shown to neighbor. Here then the prayer shows the couple that with blessings comes the social responsibility to share. The idea of their own marriage "sacramentalizing" or mirroring the faithfulness and generosity of God is thus implied.

The flowers are described to have come from paradise in order to remind them of the first couple, Adam and Eve. Eden, which these flowers recall, signifies many things. It reminds the couple of the life of happiness and peace which our first parents enjoyed. But it recalls also their fall from grace. The flowers then serve as an encouragement and a warning. They are encouraged by the knowledge that their marriage is in God's plan and God's desire for them is their happiness. But they are also cautioned that when they lose sight of God and listen only to their own selfish selves they are bound to fall.

THANKSGIVING AT THE HOME ALTAR (ALABADO)

Once inside the house, the couple kneel before the altar. A designated *mangluluало* or prayer leader proceeds to recite some prayers for the couple. The following is proposed for use on this occasion:[7]

"My brothers and sisters, let us now pray for N. and N. as they begin their married life together. After each petition please respond: (LORD) HEAR US.

"Most loving God, bless and bring good fortune to N. and N. and the family they are going to build. We ask you, Lord.

"Grant them the abundant fruits of the dew from heaven and the richness of the earth as you gave Isaac and his wife Rebecca. We ask you, Lord.

"Grant them genuine love and patience for one another that they may remain faithful to each other at all times. We ask you, Lord.

"Bless them with children who will strengthen the bond of love between them, children who are good, intelligent and holy who will be their consolation in time of suffering and their refuge in their old age. We ask you, Lord.

"Guide them always so that everything they say and do will always conform to your will, and may they learn compassion and generosity in sharing the blessings they receive, especially with the poor. We ask you, Lord."

Obviously, the contents of the prayers are quite similar to the prayer formulas we have reviewed so far. They ask for success for the couple's married life *(pammagasat)*, mutual love, and patience. The gift or blessing of children is mentioned but specifies the qualities that these should have; namely, good, mature, responsible, intelligent, and holy, well-mannered. The reference to children as the consolation of parents in time of suffering or trial and refuge in their old age points to the tradition among Ilocanos that the children see it as their grave duty never to neglect their parents in their time of need and to take care of them in their old age. To do otherwise is considered a curse. The last petition asks for the Lord's guidance over the couple and that they may also learn compassion and generosity. This echoes one of the prayers in the solemn blessing indicating their social responsibility as a part of the fulfillment of their vocation as married disciples.

---

[7] This formula draws some inspiration from the prayers found in Mariano Pacis, *Ti Panagrosario ken Dagiti Paka-usaranna* (Laoag City: Grace Printing Press, 1989) 46–8.

The prayers may be concluded with the recitation or singing of the Lord's Prayer. In some places an *alabado,* a song of praise and thanksgiving, addressed either to God or to the Blessed Virgin Mary, is sung after common prayers. It would be appropriate at this time to sing such a song or another hymn that expresses gratitude and praise for the Lord's gift of marriage. In the course of the singing the couple could offer a bouquet of flowers to the altar where the images are placed.

THE WEDDING BANQUET

To maintain the religious character of the wedding celebration it behooves that a prayer be said before the couple and the rest of the guests start partaking of the feast. To make everyone aware of the gospel exhortation to have concern for the needy while they dine, dance, and party, the text from the book of Tobit (4:16, 18-19) may be proclaimed before the grace before meals is said. The prayer leader (one of the parents, godparents, elder, or lay minister) reads: "Give to the hungry some of your bread, and to the naked some of your clothing. . . . Seek counsel from every wise man, and do not think lightly of any advice that can be useful. At all times bless the Lord, and ask him to make all your paths straight and to grant success to all your endeavors and plans." After proclaiming the text he proceeds to the prayer of blessing either with the following text or something similar:

"Blessed are you, O Lord, for in your great providence you have given us these food and drink we are to share on this happy occasion of N. and N. marriage. May the food renew our strength, give energy to our bodies, and new thought to our minds. May this drink restore our souls, give vision and joy to our spirits, and warmth to the love in our hearts. And once refreshed, may we use our whole selves, mind and body, heart and spirit to proclaim your great glory and to serve our brethren. Amen."

This is a simple prayer that starts off with blessing God for the gifts of food and drink. It then petitions that they be the sources of renewed strength, energy, and joy to body, mind, and spirit, as well as warmth to the love in the heart. It goes on to add the duty to thank and proclaim God's glory as well as of service to others. Other formulas of course may always be used.

The wedding cake and its attending ritual is an example of Western influence on the Ilocano culture. It is fast becoming a common element in wedding celebrations. Just because it is not an original Ilocano tradition should not be a reason to suppress the practice. In itself it is a good ritual and could very well be adapted to the Ilocano culture.

The sharing of food between the bride and the groom is one of the truly ancient and consistently universal symbols enacted at a wedding ceremony. It reflects the sharing of food and drink in communion. It makes of the two "companions for life" in the sense that companion has the meaning of "the one with whom you share your bread/food." This is underscored in cutting the wedding cake together and feeding each other a piece of it. Feeding each other a piece of the cake symbolizes the ways in which they will nourish and share with each other in their life together as a couple.

By further sharing the cake with the guests, it invites the entire group to become companions in the sharing of this food. It is intimacy and an invitation to community all in a single sign. By the same token, in sharing the couple's cake the guests have also accepted responsibility over the couple. Having "broken cake" with them in time of joy they are making a pledge to be ready to assist them whenever they are in sorrow, suffering, or need.

To bring out the religious dimension of this cake ritual it would be nice to have somebody (either one of the parents, godparents, elders, friends of the couple) say a short blessing while inviting all the guests to participate by extending a hand in the direction of the couple. One of the formulas for solemn blessings (such as the one from Num 6:24-26, the blessings of Aaron)[8] may be used. Or perhaps one can use the following text:

"May the blessings of our loving God rest upon you and remain with you.

"May the Lord's peace abide with you.

"May God's presence in your midst illuminate your hearts now and forevermore."

An alternative prayer would be something that expresses gratitude for the couple, the meal, and the joy that is shared by all.

[8] The text reads, "The Lord bless you and keep you! The Lord let his face shine upon you and be gracious to you! The Lord look upon you kindly and give you peace!" (Num 6:24-26).

POST-WEDDING OBSERVANCES

The day following the wedding is a time of thanksgiving. The new couple rises early to go to church, take part in the Mass, and offer prayers of gratitude. This is also a day when the dead relatives of both parties are honored and remembered through prayers and a simple party, either at the house of the bridegroom or the bride, depending on where the wedding reception was held.

Before lunch is served prayers are offered on behalf of the dead. The local *manglulualo* or the community's prayer leader, usually a woman, may be called upon to preside over the activity. The recitation of the rosary, because of its popularity among the people, should be preserved. But there is a need to revise the prayers for the dead which most of the people are using because the texts and the theology behind them are quite outdated.[9] Perhaps one possibility is to use the Office for the Dead found in the Liturgy of the Hours or in the Order of Christian Funerals.[10]

Before they start offering prayers for the dead, samples of food may likewise be set aside as a food offering *(atang)* for the dead. There is nothing superstitious about this; it is simply a way, as at funerals, of expressing the communion that still exists between the living and the dead. On all major occasions in Ilocano society, the presence of the living dead is symbolized and acknowledged in this fashion.

After all these ceremonies, the couple is ready to embark on married life together, with their own partnership now forged and blessed, but without breaking the bonds or ties that exist between them and their families, and between them and the dead. The services as we have presented them here can enable them to imbibe a good sense of their own cultural heritage, doing so, however, within the Christian vision that is the abiding reality of Christian marriage ceremonies and traditions.

---

[9] One source of the prayer texts is a pamphlet bearing the title *Novena a Pangicacaasi Cadagiti Bendito a Cararua Sadi Purgatorio* (Vigan: El Tiempo Catolico, 1940). There is no author specified. The cover page simply indicates that it was written by an Augustinian friar. It was probably first published during the Spanish era but had been continuously reprinted.

[10] See for example, Order of Christian Funerals approved for use in the dioceses of the United States of America by the National Conference of Catholic Bishops and confirmed by the Apostolic See (New York: Catholic Book Publishing Co., 1989) 303–26.

CONCLUSION

The work of preparing a contextualized Ilocano Marriage Rite has been illustrated in this chapter, based on the complete text which the author has put together. What has not been discussed here at length is the work of translation from Latin texts, the choice of scriptural texts, and the selection of appropriate music and chant. The purpose here was to simply illustrate the nature of the task by focusing on some of the more culturally rooted aspects of engagement, marriage preparation, and wedding celebration.

Bibliography

LITURGICAL DOCUMENTS

Ang Pagdiriwang ng Pag-iisang Dibdib. Salin sa Tagalog ng Huwarang Sipi. Manila: Panayam ng mga Katolikong Obispo ng Pilipinas, Lupon para sa Wikang Tagalog sa Liturhiya, 1983.

Baumgartner, Jakob. *Mission und Liturgie in Mexiko.* Vol. 2: *Die Ersten Liturgischen Bücher in der Neuen Welt.* Schoeneck/Beckenried: NZM, 1972.

Benedictionale: Rituale romanum ex decreto sacrosancti Œcumenici Concilii Vaticani II instauratum auctoritate Ioannis Pauli II promulgatum. Editio typica. Urbs Vaticana: Typis Polyglottis Vaticanis, 1985.

Bishops' Committee on the Liturgy. *Catholic Household Blessings and Prayers.* Washington, D.C.: United States Catholic Conference, 1988.

Catholic Bishops' Conference of the Philippines. *Marriage Rite for the Philippines.* Manila: Catholic Trade School, 1973.

Collectio Rituum. Ed. Moises Andrade. Manila: Archdiocese of Manila, 1983.

Congregatio de Cultu Divino et Disciplina Sacramentorum. "De Liturgia Romana et Inculturatione. Instructio Quarta 'Ad Exsecutionem Constitutionis Concilii Vaticani Secundi de Sacra Liturgia Recte Ordinandam' (Ad Const. Art. 37–40)." *Notitiae* XXX (1994) 80–115.

Congregation for Divine Worship and the Discipline of the Sacraments. *The Roman Liturgy and Inculturation.* Fourth Instruction for the Right Application of the Conciliar Constitution on the Liturgy, nos. 37–40. Rome: Vatican Press, 1994.

De Mentrida, Fray Alonso. *Ritual para administrar los santos sacramentos, sacado casi todo del Ritual Romano, y lo demás del Ritual Indico.* Manila: Imprenta de la Compaña de Jesus, 1630.

International Commission on English in the Liturgy. *The Sacramentary.* New York: Catholic Book Publishing Co., 1985.

Kaczynski, Reiner. *Enchiridion Documentorum Instaurationis Liturgicae, 2.* Rome: Marietti, 1988.

Le Sacramentaire Grégorien. Ed. Jean Deshusses, Spicilegium Friburgense 16. Fribourg, 1971.

Le Liber Ordinum en usage dans l'église wisigothique et mozarabe d'Espagne du cinquième au onzième siècle. Ed. M. Férotin. Mon. eccles. lit. 5. Paris: Firmin-Didot, 1904.

Order of Christian Funerals. Approved for use in the dioceses of the United States of America by the National Conference of Catholic Bishops and confirmed by the Apostolic See. New York: Catholic Book Publishing Co., 1989.

Ordo Celebrandi Matrimonium. Editio Typica. Vatican City: Typis Polyglottis, 1969.

Ordo Celebrandi Matrimonium. Editio Typica Altera. Vatican City: Typis Polyglottis, 1990.

Rituale Romanum Pauli V pontificis maximi iussu editum. Rome: 1614.

Rituale Romanum, Rito ti Santa Iglesia iti Panangcasar Ditoy Filipinas, approbatum a Coetu Episcoporum Regionis Ilocanae. Vigan: Ilocano Interdiocesan Liturgical Commission, 1970.

Ritzer, Korbinian. _Formen, riten und religiöses Brachtum der Eheschliessung in den christlichen Kirchen des estern Jahrtausends,_ Liturgiewissenschaftliche Quellen und Forschungen 38. Münster: Aschendorf, 1962.

_____. _Le mariage dans les églises chrétiennes._ Paris: Les Éditions du Cerf, 1970.

Sacramentarium Fuldense Saeculi X. Ed. G. Richter and A. Schönfelder. Fulda: Abtei Fulda, 1912.

Searle, Mark, and Kenneth Stevenson, eds. _Documents of the Marriage Liturgy._ Collegeville: The Liturgical Press, 1992.

Tanner, Norman. _Decrees of the Ecumenical Councils._ Vol. II. London/Washington, D.C.: Sheed and Ward/Georgetown University Press, 1990.

LITERATURE ON THE RITES OF MARRIAGE

OCM 1969

Boggio, G. "Temi biblici nel lezionario del matrimonio." _Rivista Liturgica_ 63 (1976) 529–51.

Braga, C. "La genesi dell 'Ordo Matrimonii.'" _Ephemerides Liturgicae_ 93 (1979) 247–57.

Brovelli, F. "La celebrazione del matrimonio. Analisi del nuovo rituale." _Rivista Liturgica_ 63 (1976) 500–28.

Cardinali, B. "Il rito del matrimonio nel processo delle culture." _Rivista Liturgica_ 63 (1976) 467–99.

Carideo, C. "Teología della celebrazione liturgica del matrimonio cristiano." _La celebrazione del matrimonio cristiano._ 163–202. Bologna: Edizioni Dehoniane, 1977.

Farnedi, G., ed. _La celebrazione cristiana del matrimonio._ Studia Anselmiana 93; Analecta 11. Rome: Pontificio Ateneo S. Anselmo, 1986.

Gy, Pierre-Marie. "Le nouveau rituel romain du mariage." *La Maison-Dieu* 99 (1969) 124–43.

Lukken, Gerard. "Relevance of Semiotic Analysis to the Liturgical Sciences Illustrated in the Light of the Rite of Marriage." *Per Visibilia ad Invisibilia.* Ed. Louis van Tongeren and Charles Caspers, 299–310. Kampen: Kok Pharos Publishing, 1994.

_____. "Die Stellung der Frau im Trauungsritus des Rituale Romanum und nach Vaticanum II. Von der Unterordnung der Frau zu einer gewissen Gleichwertigkeit von Mann und Frau." *Per Visibilia ad Invisibilia.* Ed. Louis van Tongeren and Charles Caspers, 311–34. Kampen: Kok Pharos Publishing, 1994.

Molin, J. B. "Symboles, rites et textes du mariage au Moyen Age Latin." *La celebrazione cristiana del matrimonio.* Ed. G. Farnedi, 107–27. Studia Anselmiana 93; Analecta 11. Rome: Pontificio Ateneo S. Anselmo, 1986.

Nocent, A. "Il matrimonio cristiano." *Anamnesis: Introduzione storico-teologica alla liturgia.* Vol. 3:1 (Rome: Marietti, 1986) 348–50.

_____. "Le rituel du mariage depuis Vatican II." *La celebrazione cristiana del matrimonio.* Ed. G. Farnedi, 129–44. Studia Anselmiana 93; Analecta 11. Rome: Pontificio Ateneo S. Anselmo, 1986.

Serrano, Ricardo. "Towards a Cultural Adaptation of the Rite of Marriage." Unpublished S.L.D. dissertation. Rome: Pontifical Institute of Liturgy, 1987.

Stevenson, Kenneth. *To Join Together: The Rite of Marriage.* New York: Pueblo Publishing, 1987.

_____. *Nuptial Blessing: A Study of Christian Marriage Rites.* Alcuin Club Collections 64. London: SPCK, 1982.

_____. "The Origins of Nuptial Blessing." *Heythrop Journal* 21 (1980) 412–6.

Triacca, A. M. "Celebrare il matrimonio cristiano: Suo significato teologico-liturgico." *Ephemerides Liturgicae* 93 (1979) 407–56.

_____. "La celebrazione del matrimonio: Aspetti teologico-liturgici." *Realtá e valori del sacramento del matrimonio.* Atti del congresso di aggiornamento organizatto della Facoltá di teologia dell UPS. Ed. A. M. Triacca and G. Pianazzi, 103–50. Rome: Libreria Ateneo Salesiana, 1976.

Ward, Anthony, and Cuthbert Johnson. "The Sources of the Roman Missal (1975) II: Prefaces." *Notitiae* 23 (1987) 859–74.

ROCM 1990

Borobio, Dionisio Garcia. *Inculturación del matrimonio. Ritos y custombres matrimoniales de ayer y hoy.* Madrid: San Pablo, 1993.

_____. "Matrimonio e inculturación en la liturgia de la iglesia occidental." *Salmaticensis* 40 (1993) 271–97.

Cecolin, R. "Il lezionario del nuovo 'Ordo Celebrandi Matrimonium': Alcune annotazioni di carattere biblico-liturgico." *Rivista Liturgica* 79 (1992) 635–58.

Joncas, Jan Michael. "Solemnizing the Mystery of Wedded-Love: Nuptial Blessings in the 'Ordo Celebrandi Matrimonium 1991.'" *Worship* 70 (1996) 210–37.

Lodi, Enzo. "La Benedizione nuzziale: Sua valenza teologico-liturgica." *Rivista Liturgica* 79 (1992) 659–91.

Lopez, Julian. "La segunda edición del ritual del matrimonio: Aspectos teológicos y pastorales." *Phase* 203 (1994) 403–18.

Martinez, German. *Worship: Wedding to Marriage*. Washington, D.C.: Pastoral Press, 1993.

Nocent, Adrien. "La nouvelle édition du rituel du marriage." *Ecclesia Orans* VIII (1991) 330–4.

Rodriguez, José M. "Nueva edición del ritual del matrimonio." *Phase* 187 (1992) 13–26.

Sacred Congregation on Divine Worship. "Commentarium on the ROCM." *Notitiae* 26 (1990) 310–27.

Triacca, A. M. "Spiritus Sancti vitutis infuzio: A proposito di alcune tematiche teologico-liturgiche testimoniale nell 'editio altera' dell 'Ordo Celebrandi Matrimonium.'" *Notitiae* 26 (1990) 365–90.

———. "Linee teologico-liturgici in vista di una rinnovata celebrazione del matrimonio." *Rivista Liturgica* 79 (1992) 599–634.

LITERATURE ON LITURGICAL INCULTURATION AND CONTEXTUALIZATION

Agnelo, Geraldo. "Liturgia Romana e inculturazione." *Notitiae* XXX (1994) 71–7.

Antonio, William David. "Developing a Funeral Liturgy Among the Ilocano People of the Philippines." Unpublished S.T.L. dissertation. Washington, D.C.: Catholic University of America, 1993.

Bevans, Stephen. *Models of Contextual Theology*. Maryknoll, N.Y.: Orbis Books, 1992.

Borobio, Dionisio. "Matrimonio e inculturación en la liturgia de la iglesia occidental." *Salmaticensis* 40 (1993) 271–97.

———. *Inculturación del matrimonio*. Madrid: San Pablo, 1993.

Canals, Joel M. "Realizaciones de inculturación en la liturgia romana." *Phase* XXXV (1995) 113–26.

Chupungco, Anscar. *Cultural Adaptation of the Liturgy*. New York: Paulist Press, 1982.

———. "The Cultural Adaptation of the Rite of Marriage." *La celebrazione cristiana del matrimonio*. Ed. G. Farnedi, 145–62. Studia Anselmiana 93; Analecta 11. Rome: Pontificio Ateneo S. Anselmo, 1986.

———. "A Definition of Liturgical Inculturation." *Ecclesia Orans* 5 (1988) 11–23.

_____. "Inculturation and the Organic Progression of the Liturgy." *Ecclesia Orans* 7 (1990) 7–21.

_____. "Liturgical Inculturation." *East Asian Pastoral Review* 30 (1993) 108–19.

_____. *Liturgical Inculturation: Sacramentals, Religiosity, and Catechesis.* Collegeville: The Liturgical Press, 1992.

_____. *Liturgies of the Future: The Process and Methods of Inculturation.* Mahwah, N.J.: Paulist Press, 1989.

_____. "Popular Religiosity and Liturgical Inculturation." *Ecclesia Orans* 8 (1991) 97–115.

_____. "Remarks on 'The Roman Liturgy and Inculturation.'" *Ecclesia Orans* 11 (1994) 269–77.

De Mesa, José. *Following the Way of the Disciples.* Quezon City: East Asian Pastoral Institute, 1996.

_____. *In Solidarity with the Culture.* Quezon City: Maryhill School of Theology, 1987.

_____. *Marriage Is Discipleship.* Quezon City: East Asian Pastoral Institute, 1995.

_____. "Marriage Is Discipleship 1." *East Asian Pastoral Review* 28 (1991) 313–96.

_____. "Marriage Is Discipleship 2." *East Asian Pastoral Review* 29 (1992) 3–107.

De Mesa, José, and L. Wostyn. *Doing Theology.* Quezon City: Claretian Publications, 1990.

Irwin, Kevin W. *Context and Text: Method in Liturgical Theology.* Collegeville: The Liturgical Press, 1994.

Jounel, Pierre. "Une étape majeure sur le chemin de l'inculturation liturgique." *Notitiae* XXX (1994) 260–77.

Luzbetak, Louis. *The Church and Cultures: New Perspectives in Missiology.* Maryknoll, N.Y.: Orbis Books, 1988.

Martin, Kenneth J. "Genetic and Analytic Study of the 'Roman Liturgy and Inculturation: Fourth Instruction for the Right Application of the Conciliar Constitution on the Liturgy (nos. 37–40).'" Unpublished S.T.L. thesis. Washington, D.C.: Catholic University of America, 1996.

Mercado, Leonardo. *Christ in the Philippines.* Tacloban City: Divine Word University Publications, 1982.

_____. *Doing Filipino Theology.* Manila: Divine Word Publications, 1997.

_____. *Elements of Filipino Theology.* Tacloban City: Divine Word University Publications, 1975.

_____. *Inculturation and Filipino Theology.* Manila: Divine Word Publications, 1992.

Miranda, Dionisio M. *Buting Pinoy: Probe Essays on Value as Filipino.* Manila: Divine Word Publications, 1992.

_____. "Fragments of a Method of Inculturation." *East Asian Pastoral Review* 30 (1993) 145–67.

_____. "Inculturation and Moral Theology." *Philippiniana Sacra* XXVIII (1993) 289–309.

_____. "Outlines of a Method of Inculturation." *East Asian Pastoral Review* 30 (1993) 145–67.

Rocha, Pedro. "Liturgia e inculturazione (Dalla Const. *Sacrosanctum Concilium* [SC] all'istruzione *Varietates legitimae* [VL])." *Studia Missionalia* 44 (1995) 149–68.

Sacred Congregation on Divine Worship. "'Commentariu' alla quarta istruzione per una corretta applicazione della costituzione conciliare sulla sacra liturgia." *Notitiae XXX* (1994) 152–66.

Schreiter, Robert. *Constructing Local Theologies.* Maryknoll, N.Y.: Orbis Books, 1985.

Ukpong, Justin. "Contextualization: Concept and History." *Revue Africaine de Théologie* 2 (1987) 148–63.

Yáñez, José L. "La inculturación en la liturgia: Comentario desde América." *Phase XXXV* (1995) 135–42.

LITERATURE ON ETHNOGRAPHY/HISTORY OF FILIPINO CULTURE

Anima, Nid. *Ilocandia: Land of Contrasts and Contradictions.* Quezon City: Omar Publications, 1976.

Arce, W. F. "Godfathership." *Filipino Heritage: The Making of a Nation.* Vol. IV. Ed. A. Roces, 1020–1. Manila: Lahing Pilipino Publishing, 1978.

Balquiedra, Luis. "The Liturgical Principles Used by the Missionaries and the Missionary Background to the Christianization of the Philippines." *Philippiniana Sacra XXX* (1995) 5–79.

_____. "The New Order of Worship for Native Filipinos." *Philippiniana Sacra XXX* (1995) 185–250.

Barrion, Maria Caridad. "Religious Life of the Laity in Eighteenth-Century Philippines." *Boletin Ecclesiastico de Filipinas XXXIV*, Nos. 385–90 (July–December 1960) 426–38, 490–501, 552–65, 698–708, 763–73.

_____. "Religious Life of the Laity in Eighteenth-Century Philippines." *Boletin Ecclesiastico de Filipinas XXV*, Nos. 391–3 (January–March 1961) 43–51, 107–14, 158–70.

Beyer, H. Otley. "Outline Review of Philippine Archaeology by Islands and Provinces." *Philippine Journal of Science LXXVII* (July–August 1947) 205–390.

_____. "Philippine and East Asian Archaeology and Its Relation to the Origins of the Pacific Islands Population." *National Research Council Bulletin* 29 (1948).

Blair, Emma Helen, and James Alexander Robertson, eds. *History of the Philippine Islands 1493–1898.* Vols. V, VII, XII, XL, and XLII. Cleveland: A. H. Clark Company, 1903–09.

Calip, José Resurrección. "The Iloko Epic, Lam-ang." Unpublished Ph.D. dissertation. Manila: University of Santo Tomas, 1957.

Chirino, Pedro. *Relación de las Islas Filipinas*. Trans. Ramon Echavarria. Manila: Historical Conservation Society, 1969.

De la Costa, Horacio. *Readings in Philippine History*. Makati: Bookmark, 1965.

Demetrio, Francisco. *Encyclopedia of Philippine Folk Beliefs and Customs*. Vol. II. Cagayan de Oro: Xavier University, 1991.

Dolan, Ronald, ed. *Philippines: A Country Study*. 4th ed. Area Handbook Series. Washington, D.C.: Federal Research Division, Library of Congress, 1993.

Dumlao, Alejandro. "Ancient Marriage Customs Among the Ilocanos." *The College Folio* I (February 1911) 135–41.

Foronda, Juan A. "The Establishment of the First Missionary Centers in Ilocos (1572–1612)." *Ilocos Review* III (1971) 1–75.

Gagelonia, Pedro. *The Filipinos of Yesteryears*. Manila: National Bookstore, 1973.

García, Excelso. "Particular Discipline on Marriage in the Philippines During the Spanish Regime." *Philippiniana Sacra* VIII (January–April 1973) 7–85.

Garcia, Miguel, "Relación del estado de la iglesia de Nueva Segovia en las Islas Filipinas, remitida al Rey y Supremo Consejo de Indias." *Archivo de la Provincia del Santisimo Rosario* (September 20, 1774) Tomo 7, Doc. 13, Cap. 8, no. 4.

Geertz, Clifford. *Interpretation of Cultures*. New York: Basic Books, 1973.

Gloria, Heidi. "Ethnohistory, Ethnicity, and the Problem of Filipino Identity." *Tambara: The Ateneo de Davao University Journal* II (December 1985) 2–13.

Gutiérrez, Lucio. "The Evangelization of the Philippines and the Formative Years of the Archdiocese of Manila (1565–1700)." *Philippiniana Sacra* XXX (1995) 373–424.

Hislop, Stephen K. "Anitism: A Survey of Religious Beliefs Native to the Philippines." *Asian Studies* 9 (August 1971) 144–56.

Jocano, F. Landa. "Beyer's Theory on Filipino Prehistory and Culture: An Alternative Approach to the Problem." *Studies in Philippine Anthropology: In Honor of H. Otley Beyer*. Ed. Mario Zamora, 128–50. Quezon City: Alemar Publishers, 1967.

_____. *Growing Up in a Philippine Barrio*. New York: Holt, Rinehart and Winston, 1969.

_____. *The Ilocanos: An Ethnography of Family and Community Life in the Ilocos Region*. Quezon City: Asian Center, 1982.

Karnow, Stanley. *In Our Image: America's Empire in the Philippines*. New York: Ballantine Books, 1989.

Magbag, Crescencio. "The Topak in the Ilokano Wedding." *Philippine Magazine* 32 (January 1935) 33.

Nieto, Marcelino. "The Work of the Augustinians in Ilokos." *Ilocos Review* III (1971) 166–226.

Nydegger, William, and Corinne Nydegger. *Tarong: An Ilocos Barrio in the Philippines*. Ed. Beatrice Whiting. Six Culture Series VI. New York: John Wiley and Sons, 1966.

Pacis, Mariano. *Ti Panag-rosario ken Dagiti Paka-usaranna.* Laoag City: Grace Printing Press, 1989.

Phelan, John Leddy. *The Hispanization of the Philippines: Spanish Aims and Responses.* Madison: University of Wisconsin Press, 1959.

_____. "Prebaptismal Instruction and the Administration of Baptism in the Philippines During the Sixteenth Century." *Studies in Philippine Church History.* Ed. Gerald H. Anderson, 22–43. Ithaca, N.Y./London: Cornell University Press, 1969.

Picornell, P. *The Philippine Chronicles of Fray San Antonio.* Manila: Historical Conservation Society, 1977.

Quisumbing, Lourdes. *Marriage Customs in Rural Cebu.* Cebu City: San Carlos Publications, 1965.

Reyno, Rodulfo. "Customary Wedding Among the Ilocanos." *Philippine Magazine* 35 (July 1939) 336, 346, 348.

Scheans, Daniel. "The Ilocano: Marriage and the Land." *Philippine Sociological Review* XI (June–October 1963) 216–35.

Scott, William Henry. "Filipino Class Structure in the Sixteenth Century." *Cracks in the Parchment Curtain and Other Essays in Philippine History.* 96–126. Quezon City: New Day Publishers, 1982.

_____. *Prehispanic Source Materials for the Study of Philippine History.* Quezon City: New Day Publishers, 1984.

_____. "Visayan Religion at the Time of Spanish Advent." *Philippiniana Sacra* XXV (1990) 397–415.

Somera, Rene. "Marriage and the Ilocano Oldtimer." *Philippine Studies* 34 (1986) 181–99.

Sturtevant, William. "Anthropology, History, and Ethnohistory." *Introduction to Cultural Anthropology.* Ed. James Clifton, 451–75. Boston: Houghton Mifflin Company, 1968.

Tylor, Edward Burnett. *Religion in Primitive Culture.* Rev. ed. New York: Harper Brothers Publishers, 1958.

Valera, Edmundo. "Theology of Struggle: The Philippines' Ecclesial Experience." *New Theology Review* 5 (May 1992) 62–85.

OTHER SOURCES

Acts of the Synod of Calasiao (1773). Trans. Ma. Benita de los Reyes. *Philippiniana Sacra* V (1970) 74–229.

Acts and Decrees of the Second Plenary Council of the Philippines. 20 January–17 February 1991. Manila: Catholic Bishops' Conference of the Philippines, 1992.

Acts and Decrees of the First Nueva Segovia Pastoral Assembly. 11–17 April 1993. Vigan: Archdiocese of Nueva Segovia, 1993.

A New Heart and a New Spirit. Northern Luzon Pastoral Forum I Papers, Baguio City. 23–27 September 1996. Baguio City: Northern Luzon Bishops' Conference, 1997.

Code of Canon Law. Latin-English Edition. Washington, D.C.: Canon Law Society of America, 1983.

Constantino, Ernesto. *Ilokano Dictionary.* Honolulu: University of Hawaii Press, 1971.

Denzinger, H., and A. Schönmetzer, eds. *Enchiridion Symbolorum, Definitionum et Declarationum de Rebus Fidei et Morum.* 36th ed. Barcinone/Friburgi Brisgoviae/Rome: Herder, 1976.

Instituto de Liturgia Hispana. *Gift and Promise, Customs and Traditions in Hispanic Rites of Marriage.* Portland: Oregon Catholic Press, 1997.

Leo the Great. "Sermo XXII." *Patrologia Latina* 54:193–4.

Mackin, Theodore. *The Marital Sacrament.* New York/Mahwah, N.J.: Paulist Press, 1989.

Maynigo, Victor. "Evangelization and Philippine Culture in the Light of the Second Vatican Council." Unpublished S.T.D. dissertation. Rome: Pontifical University of St. Thomas, 1978.

Novena a Pangicacaasi Cadagiti Bendito a Cararua Sadi Purgatorio. Vigan: El Tiempo Catolico, 1940.

Pope John Paul II. Apostolic Constitution *Scripturam thesaurus. AAS* 71 (1979) 557–9.

_____. Apostolic Exhortation *Familiaris Consortio* (1980). *AAS* 74 (1982) 143–65.

_____. Apostolic Letter *Vicesimus quintus annus* (4 December 1988) 18. *AAS* 81 (1989) 912–4.

_____. Encyclical Letter *Redemptoris Missio* (7 December 1990). *AAS* 83 (1991) 300–2.

Pope Pius XI. Encyclical Letter *Casti Connubii. AAS* 22 (1930) 546–7.

Rahner, Karl. *Foundations of Christian Faith.* Trans. William Dych. New York: Seabury Press, 1978.

_____. "How to Receive a Sacrament and Mean It." *Theology Digest* 19 (August 1971) 227–34.

The Family Code of the Philippines. Executive Order No. 209, As Amended by E.O. No. 227. Manila: National Bookstore, 1988.

Vogel, Cyrille. *The Medieval Liturgy: An Introduction to the Sources.* Trans. and rev. W. Storey and N. Rasmussen. Washington, D.C.: Pastoral Press, 1986.

Index